WATCHER IN THE SHADOW

A Play

NORMAN HOLLAND

SAMUEL FRENCH

LONDON

NEW YORK SYDNEY TORONTO HOLLYWOOD

ISBN 0 573 03019 7

Printed in Great Britain by W & J Mackay Limited, Chatham

WATCHER IN THE SHADOW

Characters:

Janey Johnson, a housekeeper
Kesiah, a gipsy
Margaret Sumner
Nelly, a servant
Dr Helen Graham
Ellen Walsh, an applicant
Rose Farnley, a gossip
Deborah Barker
Emmeline Martell

The action passes in the housekeeper's room in the Old Manor House, near Retford, Kent, on the fringe of the Romney Marshes

Time—1908

**For Marian and Frank
with love**

WATCHER IN THE SHADOW

ACT I

SCENE 1

The Housekeeper's Room in the Old Manor House, Retford, Kent. An evening in early July, 1908

The room is something less than a luxurious apartment. The house is on the fringe of the Romney Marshes and something of the bleakness of the Marshes has communicated itself to the room. In the rear wall is a door—usually open, and which is well L *of* C, *with a passage beyond it. A person leaving the room through the door would turn* L *to the (invisible) outer door, which opens on the yard, or* R *to reach the rest of the house. Inside the room is a dresser which accommodates the best china, which is kept separate from the kitchen ware.* R *of the door is a line of coat hooks with a shopping bag hanging from one of them. Beyond the coat hooks is a window which affords a glimpse of the yard outside. In the* R *wall is the door to the cellar which opens upstage. Above the cellar door is a cupboard. On the opposite wall is the fireplace, with a single worn armchair turned towards the fire which burns in the grate throughout the action of the play. There is a small table* RC *with a kitchen chair on either side of it. There are a couple of framed prints of poor quality on the walls, and the wallpaper has seen considerable service*

When the CURTAIN *rises it is dark outside. Illumination is provided by an overhead gas fitting, and the gas-light seems to emphasize the general shabbiness of the room. It seems an appropriate setting for Janey Johnson, the housekeeper. Janey is dressed with a severity which at once stresses the fact that she is middle-aged, and reflects her station in life. A bunch of keys hangs from her belt. She is seated in the armchair, but is clearly ill at ease. She glances in the direction of the window, realizes that she cannot see outside from where she is sitting, and goes over to the window, where she peers into the darkness. After a moment she exclaims briefly, goes out of the room and turns* L. *We hear her unlatch the unseen outer door. Hereafter, throughout the play, this door is heard to open and close as necessary to the action*

Janey (*off*) Is that you, Kesiah? Kesiah . . . Don't stand there. Come inside.

Janey returns to the room preceding Kesiah, a striking-looking gipsy about her own age. Kesiah wears ear-rings, a colourful head-scarf and her well-

worn clothes have a flamboyant brightness which contrast sharply with the shabby surroundings. She carries a thong, one end of which is wound round her wrist. The gipsy seems pleased to be indoors and glances about her appreciatively

Janey You frightened me, Kesiah. I could only just see your face in the dark. When I looked out, I thought I saw Death himself standing there.

Kesiah I was standing in the shadow. (*She walks over to the armchair, unwinds the thong from her wrist and casually drapes it over the chair-back*) You do well to be afraid, Janey. Cleo, an old woman of our tribe, read my hand long ago and warned me to beware of the watcher in the shadow. (*Then, reacting to Janey's expression of alarm*) Don't be foolish, Janey. Here's only your old friend, Kesiah, come to pay you the promised visit.

Janey She's come back, Kesiah. The mistress has come back.

Kesiah (*frowning angrily*) Come back, has she? Does that mean I can't stay?

Janey (*hastily*) No, no. I've made it all right with her—though it wasn't easy. I've told her that there was a chance you would be coming today— but I wasn't really expecting you until tomorrow. You can stay in the gardener's cottage.

Kesiah The gardener's cottage!

Janey You'll be snug in there, Kesiah.

Kesiah It hasn't been lived in for months—not since old Miles went.

Janey (*pleading*) It's the best I could do—and I have aired the bed.

Kesiah I should hope so.

Janey Mrs Sumner doesn't like gipsies. I had to beg her to . . .

Kesiah Doesn't like gipsies, eh? None of them like gipsies—not until they need one. Where is she now?

Janey In her drawing room and she'll stay there. She won't trouble us. She'll be going to bed soon. Come and sit down. You must be tired.

Kesiah allows herself to be led to one of the chairs beside the table. Gratefully, she sits down

Kesiah Yes, I'm tired. (*She stretches luxuriously*) Tired to death of the roads. Since I last saw you, Janey, I've tramped a wilderness of miles.

Janey Poor Kesiah!

Kesiah Poor Kesiah, indeed! To no purpose, though. In one place I've begged a bite and a sup. In another I've sold baskets or pegs or told fortunes to earn a few miserable pence. I've lived for two days together on turnips pulled from a farmer's field. Ah, it's a dog's life!

Janey I'm so sorry, Kesiah. Can I get you some bread and cheese?

Kesiah Bread and cheese! I fared better than that the last time I was here.

Janey I keep telling you—Mrs Sumner is home I daren't give you anything else. (*Then, relenting before Kesiah's injured expression*) I'll bring you something tasty when she's gone to bed.

Kesiah (*disgustedly*) When she's gone to bed! Do we live in fear of her then?

Janey I do. When she's angry. And so would you if you worked for her. I'll get your bread and cheese.

Janey goes off to the kitchen

Kesiah looks about her speculatively

Kesiah We'd have to see about that. (*She rises*) Yes, we'd have to see which of us lived in fear—if I worked for her.

Janey comes in with a tray upon which is a glass of water and a plate of bread and cheese. Kesiah turns. Janey is halted in her tracks by the expression on Kesiah's face

Kesiah Water! You bring me water?
Janey Only until she's gone to bed, Kesiah. After that I'll bring you . . .
Kesiah No matter. Put it there.

Kesiah points arrogantly to the table. Janey hurries to the table, puts down the tray and steps back to observe Kesiah. She is awed by the gipsy's authoritative manner. Kesiah takes up the glass and raises it above her head as if it were a votive offering

Kesiah The water of affliction! (*Slowly, impressively, she lowers the glass and drinks ceremoniously. She breaks off a little of the bread and, still with an air of ceremony, eats it*) The bread of adversity! (*She replaces the glass on the tray*) These have been my portion ever since I was a girl of sixteen. It is fitting that I should eat the one and drink the other here in this place. (*Disparagingly, she surveys the room*) For I might have had a house of my own and a better one than this.

Kesiah becomes aware of Janey's amazed regard

You don't believe me, do you, Janey?
Janey (*confused*) I—I don't rightly know. You never said anything about—
Kesiah It's true, though. True as Gospel. I was born a Romany and I took the fancy of a well-to-do couple called Reardon. They adopted me and brought me up until I was sixteen. (*Proudly*) I was educated at the Brockton Young Ladies' Academy (*And it is clear that she is looking back to those days with regret*)
Janey (*timorously*) And what happened then?
Kesiah (*returning from an immense distance*) Happened?
Janey When you were sixteen?
Kesiah: A Romany whistled under my window—a lad I'd seen only twice and with whom I had spoken less than twenty words. But they were enough. When he whistled, I had to go.
Janey But you were happy? You had a good life together?
Kesiah Happy? (*She laughs bitterly*) He was weak and cruel—a wastrel. He gave me three children—two sons who will not acknowledge me and

a daughter I never want to see again. A good life! (*Again she laughs without mirth*) When the Reardons died, their lovely house was sold and they left thousands of pounds. It could have been mine—all of it—but everything went to charities. (*She sighs and turns from Janey*) I might have had a pleasant home, a loving husband and fine children if I hadn't listened to the black-browed lad under my window.

Janey goes to Kesiah and places a hand sympathetically on her arm

Janey I didn't know, Kesiah. I didn't know about this—though I always thought you too well-spoken for a gipsy.

Kesiah I don't talk about those days except when the black mood is on me. But, every night of your life, thank God kneeling that you have a roof over your head—even if it isn't your own. Thank Him that you don't lie in a ditch, a filthy barn, a stable, a cow-shed or (*scornfully*) a gardener's cottage!

Janey Kesiah, I explained to you. There was nothing I could do.

Kesiah (*her expression changing*) I know. I know. I'm being unreasonable and you're far kinder than I deserve. But I'd looked forward to a night or two of real comfort. (*Then, suddenly resolute*) One day I'll have a place of my own again. (*Nodding her head she looks about her with a calculating expression*) A place like this one.

Janey Yes, yes. Of course you will. But sit down now. You said you were tired. Eat and rest. You're wearing yourself out.

Kesiah (*sitting at the table*) All right, Janey. But you don't understand. You've always been a domestic animal. You can't imagine what it means to want something so badly that you'd do anything to get it. I want a roof over my head more than I want salvation. And I'll get it. (*She begins to eat*)

Janey Don't say things like that. You frighten me when you talk so. Eat and you'll feel better.

Kesiah That's your sovereign remedy, isn't it? But a bit of bread and cheese and a glass of water won't cure me of my troubles.

While Kesiah is speaking, Margaret Sumner, the mistress of the house, has appeared in the doorway from the kitchen. Margaret is an ageing woman with hair straggling wildly and her good clothes are worn untidily. She regards the two women unfavourably, holding on to the doorway for support

Janey I'm sorry I can't offer you anything better.

Margaret Why should you apologize for the food?

Startled, the others turn to look at her. Margaret's slurred speech and overdeliberate movements proclaim the fact that she has been drinking. She grows irritated when Janey does not reply

I said why should you apologize for the food?

Janey (*rising*) It—it seemed poor and scanty fare to offer a traveller, Mrs Sumner.

Margaret (*sarcastically*) Did it now? I've no doubt you have more lavish ideas of hospitality and you'd be pleased to indulge them if I wasn't here.

Margaret releases her grip on the door and lurches into the room. Kesiah sits as if turned to stone

But I won't have extravagance at my expense. Do you hear?

Janey (*shamed*) Yes, Mrs Sumner.

Margaret Then note it, woman! Note it! (*She points suddenly at Kesiah*) And you—sitting there eating my food. Don't you get to your feet when the mistress of the house comes into the room?

Kesiah rises

That's better. (*She turns again to Janey*) What she's eating now will be a rare banquet for her. (*To Kesiah*) Isn't it? Isn't it, now?

Kesiah remains silent. Margaret turns to Janey with a taunting expression on her face

Gipsies live on other folk's leavings: a dry crust begged at the back door, eggs filched from the farmer's hen coop, herbs cooked in a pot or, now and then, a stolen chicken or a snared rabbit. (*Abruptly wheeling on Kesiah*) Isn't that so, gipsy?

Kesiah (*struggling to maintain her composure*) If you say so, madam. If you say so.

Margaret I do say so. I know what I'm talking about. I know gipsies, too—a lying, thieving, poaching lot. (*She thrusts her face into Kesiah's*) Aren't they, gipsy?

Kesiah You claim to know the gipsies, madam.

Margaret Lazy to the backbone, that's what they are, and false as Judas. They contaminate the ground under their feet. They rob those who befriend them. But I'll tell you something, gipsy—you won't rob me!

Kesiah I am no thief, madam.

Margaret (*To Janey*) What do you think I pay you for? Go and get me a bottle of wine—red Bordeaux—from the cellar. Go on!

With a troubled, backward glance, Janey goes out by the cellar door

(*To Kesiah*) All you gipsies are thieves from birth—every last one of you. But, if you take so much as a spoon from my house, I'll have the police after you. Is that understood?

Kesiah (*nodding sombrely*) Understood.

Margaret And where did that Janey go? Where is she?

Kesiah You sent her to the cellar to get you some wine.

Margaret I know I did but I didn't tell her to be all night about it. (*Shrieking*) Janey! Janey! Hurry up! I'm waiting! (*Once more she contemplates Kesiah*) As for you . . . You'll not stay here more than one night. You'll be on your way by tomorrow afternoon. Is that clear?

Kesiah Quite clear. You have the gift of making your meaning quite plain.

Janey returns from the cellar carrying a bottle of wine. She goes over to Margaret

Margaret About time, too. Give it here. (*She examines the bottle*) This isn't what I wanted. You've got it from the wrong bin.

Janey Shall I . . .

Margaret No, no. It will have to do. You get more stupid every day. (*She starts for the kitchen door, remembers something and turns back to Kesiah*) Haven't you forgotten something?

Kesiah (*echoing*) Forgotten . . .

Margaret You haven't thanked me for my kindness in allowing you to stay here.

Kesiah But I do thank you.

Margaret And so you should.

Kesiah I am glad of the opportunity. I thank you for the warmth of your welcome, for the shelter so freely given, for the splendid repast so graciously bestowed. But, most of all, I thank you for the kindly spirit which is evident in your words and tone of voice. Such an expression touches me deeply. I shall not soon forget you.

Margaret (*suddenly plaintive*) You don't mean it. You don't mean a word of what you're saying. You're mocking me because you think I've been drinking. Oh, I can tell. There's deceit—and evil in your voice. (*Frightened, she backs to the door to the kitchen and shouts, with a return of her former manner*) Don't let me see you here after mid-day tomorrow! (*Then she rushes out screaming*) I'll be glad to see the back of you!

Margaret exits

Kesiah stands dangerously still, glaring after her. Janey goes to her and lays a restraining hand on her arm but Kesiah shakes her off roughly. The expression of hatred on Kesiah's face is terrifying as she continues to glare in the direction of the door. At length, she turns away

Kesiah I ought to wish her into a sweat. I ought to wish the sweat into a fever. I ought to curse the fever into a slow and agonizing death. That I should stand here and listen to her dispensing charity with contempt and insult. That I should stand and listen tamely! Me! (*She stamps her foot and throws back her head as she resumes the pride of bearing which she had discarded at Margaret's entrance*)

Janey (*scared*) Don't, Kesiah! Don't, I beg you!

Ignoring her, Kesiah points to the door

Kesiah I wish the cold dew on her brows, the sweat that brings with it the shivering and the tormenting ache in the bones. I wish her . . .

Janey seizes her. She drags down the extended arm and enfolds Kesiah in a desperate embrace

Janey No, no! You're not to curse her. It's the drink. She's cursed already with the drink.

Kesiah Drunk or sober, she should not have spoken so to me. (*She frees herself from Janey's but now she holds Janey and regards her curiously*) But why are you shaking?

Janey It's the stairs . . .

Kesiah Stairs?

Janey The cellar stairs. They're so steep—so awkward. I'm always afraid I'll fall. See for yourself.

Kesiah goes to the cellar door and peers downward

Kesiah They look steep all right.

Janey It's the bend—the bend in the stairs. I nearly fell just now. You won't curse her, Kesiah?

Kesiah Not this time. But I won't forget her. (*She answers abstractedly. It is obvious that her mind is elsewhere and she is thinking deeply of something else. She walks over to the armchair, takes up the thong and flexes it in her hands*)

Janey What's that? What's that you have there?

Kesiah My thong. I've always had it. Surely you've seen it before.

Janey Not that I can remember.

Kesiah Ah, now I come to think, I used to carry it wound round my waist. I've taken to carrying it—keeping it handy.

Janey Whatever for?

Kesiah A variety of uses. To keep the dogs away for a start.

By way of demonstration, she flicks out the thong in Janey's general direction. Janey leaps back in alarm

Oh, I wouldn't hurt you. But, once when I was a lot younger there was a man . . .

Janey (*suddenly interested*) Yes?

Kesiah Oh, he was drunk and had some idea that gipsy women were easy. (*She moves away from Janey and ferociously slashes left and right with the thong*) I changed his mind for him. I'll bet he stayed clear of gipsy women after I'd done with him.

Janey Put it down, Kesiah. You're frightening me again.

Kesiah (*replacing the thong on the armchair*) You're a baby, Janey. That's what you are—a baby.

Janey Sit down. Finish your bread and cheese. There's a pie in the larder. I'll get you some.

Kesiah (*sitting once more at the table*) That's better. (*She takes a drink of water and, glass in hand, nods in the direction of the kitchen*) What about her? Will she come back?

Janey Not her. She'll be in the drawing room drinking that wine. (*She sits on the chair opposite Kesiah*) She wasn't nearly as bad as this before she went up to London. It's only since she came back this last time.

Kesiah (*eating*) She went to look for her niece, didn't she?

Janey Yes. She was very upset when she didn't find her. They quarrelled bitterly and the niece went away. Mrs Sumner's been sorry ever since.

Kesiah You told me. You said something about the niece being an actress.

Janey That's right. That's what they quarrelled over. Clare—that's the niece—was offered a part and Mrs Sumner didn't think she should take it.

Kesiah She should be glad she didn't find her. (*Scornfully*) Actresses! All she says about gipsies is true about actresses. They've got the devil in their tails. Always pretending to be something they're not. They're no good to man or beast.

Janey You're wrong, Kesiah. Quite wrong about Miss Clare. She's a fine young lady.

Kesiah (*finishing the bread and cheese*) Ah, they're all the same. You can't trust any of them. Didn't you say something about a pie?

Janey Oh, yes. I'll get it.

Janey goes out into the kitchen. Kesiah is deep in thought while she is away and gives a start when Janey returns with a knife and fork and a piece of pie on a plate. Janey sets the plate, knife and fork before Kesiah

Janey There you are. You'll enjoy that—it's a game pie. (*A thought strikes her*) Just a minute . . .

Kesiah looks up expectantly and watches curiously as Janey goes to the cupboard. She pauses with her hand on the door

When I've been upset like this I—I sometimes . . .

Kesiah Yes?

Janey I sometimes take a glass of sherry.

Kesiah What a good idea.

Janey For my nerves, you understand.

Kesiah Of course.

Janey Would you join me in a glass?

Kesiah Thank you. A glass, I feel sure, would have the effect of calming my nerves.

Janey produces a bottle of sherry and two glasses from the cupboard. She brings them over to the table where she pours out two glasses of sherry and hands one to Kesiah

Janey (*raising her own glass*) Good health.

Kesiah (*rising and drinking*) Good health. (*She registers appreciation*) That's better.

Kesiah sits and, once again, Janey occupies the opposite chair. She sips her sherry and watches Kesiah as she enjoys the game pie

Janey (*at length*) You won't forget, Kesiah?

Kesiah Forget?

Janey That you're going to read my hand. To tell me about Tom—whether he thinks about me. You promised.

Kesiah If I promised, I'll read your hand.

Janey (*thrusting forward her hand*) Now? Will you read it now?

Kesiah stops eating and gives her a hard stare. Janey is intimidated and hastily withdraws her hand

When you've finished eating, of course.
Kesiah (*eating again*) Some other time.
Janey Oh, Kesiah!
Kesiah I'm too tired. It wouldn't be true—not when I'm so tired.
Janey But you will before you go?
Kesiah I've said so, haven't I? (*Suddenly irritated*) Don't pester me!

Somewhat shaken, Janey rises

Janey (*attempting to placate Kesiah*) Shall I go and make sure your room's ready while you finish your supper?
Kesiah (*readily*) Yes. Yes, please, Janey. That would be very kind of you.

Janey goes out to the kitchen

Kesiah continues to eat

After a moment or two Janey returns, carrying a lighted lantern

Janey That wretched girl! I told her twice to fill this lantern.

Kesiah rises. She is trying to conceal the fact that she is considerably disturbed—she has heard something which might upset her plans

Kesiah Girl? What girl?
Janey (*busy with the wick of the lantern*) Nelly—a girl from the village.
Kesiah Where is she?
Janey She went home this afternoon—her mother is ill.
Kesiah That's all right then. (*She is obviously relieved*)
Janey What do you mean—all right? What difference does it make whether she's here or not?
Kesiah (*sitting again*) None at all. Except that I'm never at ease with strangers.
Janey Oh, Nelly wouldn't bother you. (*She notices the bottle and glasses, puts down the lantern and approaches the table*) I'd better just put these away.

Janey removes the bottle and picks up her glass. Kesiah grabs her own glass and obviously does not intend to yield it to Janey

Kesiah Don't you trust me with the bottle then?
Janey It's just in case she should come in. Just in case . . .

Janey falters. Kesiah fixes her with an unwinking stare. She weakens and refills Kesiah's glass

There. Hide your glass if she should come back. (*She restores the bottle and glass to the cupboard*) I'll be back in a minute.

Janey exits

Kesiah watches stonily as she goes. Then she swallows the sherry at a draught, sets down the glass, and, rising, looks searchingly about the room. Her glance comes to rest on the armchair—and the thong. She goes and picks up the thong. She holds it in both hands, tautens it, snaps it experimentally

Kesiah (*nodding*) This is what is needed. This across the bend of the stairs.

Kesiah hurries to the cellar door and goes within. The room is empty for a few moments. Then Kesiah emerges and goes purposefully through the kitchen door. We hear her calling outside

Janey! Janey! Come quickly!

Kesiah backs into the room and, after a brief pause, Janey hurries in wearing a concerned expression

Janey (*as she comes in*) What is it? What's the matter?
Kesiah (*urgently*) Mrs Sumner! Down the cellar—she's calling for you. (*She takes the lantern from her*) Go on—I'll follow you with the lantern.

With Kesiah following, Janey hastens to the cellar door. As she enters, Kesiah stops abruptly just short of the door. Janey shrieks and, for a brief moment, Kesiah stands stockstill. Then, holding the lantern overhead, she goes to the cellar door and passes within. She is absent for only a matter of seconds and emerges carrying the thong which, in passing, she throws onto the armchair. At the door to the kitchen she calls out

Kesiah Mrs Sumner! Mrs Sumner! (*Still carrying the lantern, she backs towards the table*)

Margaret appears in the doorway looking disturbed and shocked into near sobriety

Margaret What is it? I heard a scream. Where's Janey?
Kesiah She went to get something from the cellar and she fell—dropped the lantern at the head of the stairs.
Margaret Go and see. Go and see what's happened to her.
Kesiah (*drawing back*) No, no. Better if you go.
Margaret You'll have to. I daren't go down there. I'll wait here.

As Kesiah still hesitates, Margaret pushes her

Hurry—she may be badly hurt.

Lantern held aloft, Kesiah goes into the cellar

Margaret goes to the door and waits. When she judges that Kesiah has reached the bottom of the stairs she calls

How is she?

There is no answer. Margaret peers down into the cellar, and backs into the room when she sees Kesiah ascending

Kesiah enters, walks over to the table and puts down the lantern

Margaret Is she badly hurt?

Kesiah She's past being hurt any more—she's dead.

Margaret Dead? Are you sure?

Kesiah (*nodding*) Quite sure. I've seen too many dead people to be mistaken.

Margaret What shall we do?

Kesiah I suppose we ought to get a doctor. Or the police. Yes, it's a police matter. Shall I go for them?

Margaret And leave me all alone with death in the house? You'll do no such thing! If we can't help Janey, she's as well where she is until morning.

Kesiah A fine mistress you are! So the floor is a fit resting place for one who has served you so well.

Margaret It doesn't matter to Janey where she lies if she's dead.

Kesiah We gipsies show respect to our dead. And what will the police say when they learn we have delayed in sending for them?

Margaret They won't know. We'll tell them we only found her in the morning.

Kesiah (*contemptuously*) And you're the one who said just now that all gipsies were liars. Would you be prepared to swear on oath that we only found her in the morning?

Margaret I don't know. I'm—I'm confused. (*Suddenly frightened*) You're not to leave me, gipsy.

Kesiah Don't call me "gipsy". I have a name. It's Kesiah.

Margaret Then stay with me, Kesiah. I have a horror of death.

Kesiah And I'm not to sleep in the gardener's cottage?

Margaret No, no. You sleep here.

Kesiah Where then?

Margaret Oh, in Janey's bed—since she won't be needing it.

Kesiah And in the morning?

Margaret Nelly will be here first thing. She can go for the police and the doctor.

Margaret turns and moves towards the kitchen but is checked when Kesiah speaks

Kesiah And then I will be free to go?

Margaret (*turning back to her*) Just as you please.

Kesiah You said I must be gone before mid-day. The gipsy will then have served her purpose. Let her take herself off and a good riddance! But I don't think I'll stay.

Margaret (*coming back to her*) You'll not stay?

Kesiah Why should I? I'll get no thanks here and I'll sleep easier in a roadside ditch than in a house of death. (*She moves as if to walk past Margaret*) I'll wish you good night.

Margaret (*clutching Kesiah*) You mustn't go! You mustn't! You can stay longer. Only don't go! I beg you not to go!

Kesiah (*freeing herself*) How long can I stay? A day? A week?

Margaret Until I get a new housekeeper.

Kesiah That's a promise?

Margaret (*nodding*) A promise.

Kesiah In that case, I might consider staying . . . (*Considering, she moves away*)

Margaret (*following her*) And when you go, I'll give you money to see you on your way.

Kesiah (*spinning round to face her*) How much? How much money?

Margaret Five pounds—five golden sovereigns.

Kesiah (*after a moment's deliberation*) I'll stay. You've made it worth my while. (*Then, menacingly*) But don't you go back on your bargain or you'll regret it.

Margaret I'll keep my word. But don't you steal away and leave me by myself.

Kesiah With a comfortable billet in prospect—and five pounds! And you claim to know all about gipsies! I'm here until the new housekeeper comes.

Margaret I'm relieved to hear it. Now I'll must move Janey's things out of her room. (*Then, noticing Kesiah's change of expression*) It's just so that you will be more comfortable. I'm moving her more personal things if you don't mind.

Kesiah Oh, I don't mind. But I hope you'll leave me one of her nightdresses. I'm very much afraid that my travelling gear doesn't include such luxuries.

Margaret I'll find you a nightdress. (*She turns again to go but pauses at the door. Reflectively*) Kesiah . . .

Kesiah Yes? Yes, what is it?

Margaret Nothing. I was just saying your name. It's a strange name . . .

Margaret goes out

Kesiah stares after her until she is out of earshot

Kesiah It will grow increasingly familiar to you as the days go by. (*She looks about the kitchen and a dawning smile reflects her change of mood*) No more lying sleepless in the wet and cold. I've done with all that. (*Still smiling, she looks up to the ceiling*) I've got a roof over my head at last. (*Her roving glance comes to rest on the empty glass and she reacts by* *going to the cupboard, opening it and taking out the bottle of sherry. She crosses to the table, fills her glass and takes it up. Smiling, she quotes)* "I sometimes take a glass of sherry . . . for my nerves, you understand." *(She laughs softly, sips the sherry with appreciation, laughs again and finishes her drink at a swallow)*

CURTAIN

SCENE 2

The same. Morning, more than two weeks later

The room is less tidy than when we saw it last. There is a tea towel draped over one of the kitchen chairs beside the table, and on the table itself there is the debris of a meal: cup and saucer, plates, milk jug, sugar basin, teapot, and a jar of marmalade. Nelly's coat hangs on one of the hooks

As the CURTAIN *rises, Nelly passes the window, then enters from the kitchen carrying some split logs which she dumps beside the fireplace. Disgustedly, hands on hips, she surveys the untidy room. She is a country girl of about twenty, roughly dressed, and dishevelled by her work. She gives a sigh of despair as she contemplates the state of the table. She takes a tray from one of the chairs, loads it up from the table and takes it into the kitchen. In a moment she returns with a cloth, with which she proceeds to wipe the table. Margaret comes in. She is less untidy, but still wears the same distraught air. She is carrying her purse*

Margaret Time's getting on, Nelly. I thought we usually had a cup of tea at this hour.

Nelly We do if I make it, ma'am. But I've so much to do these days. I never get a minute. That woman doesn't help—she makes work.

Margaret You're not to speak of her in that way. Maybe she won't be here much longer.

Nelly Amen to that. *(She makes for the kitchen with her cloth and has to pass close to Margaret)* Excuse me, ma'am. *(She goes out, and having returned the cloth to the kitchen, is back almost immediately)*

Margaret I heard what you said. I won't excuse that kind of talk. Where is Kesiah?

Nelly I haven't seen her this half hour past. She left her breakfast things on the table—as usual. She's probably upstairs resting.

Margaret At this time of day? *(Restlessly, she goes over to the dresser, runs her finger along it and then ruefully inspects its dusty tip)*

Nelly She's ready to rest any time—or to order me about. She never seems ready to work, though.

Margaret You're impudent, Nelly. Watch your tongue or I'll have to speak to your mother. How is your mother?

Nelly A bit better. Perhaps I could start living in again next week.

Margaret It would be better if you did—then I wouldn't be so dependent on Kesiah. (*On an impulse, she goes to the window leaving her purse on the dresser. She looks out*) There wasn't always such a lot of rubbish in the yard. It was different in Janey's day.

Kesiah enters quietly and stands in the doorway looking from one to the other suspiciously. She now wears a belt from which hang the bunch of keys which were Janey's badge of office. Although dressed much as we last saw her, she is better groomed and she is wearing a becoming shawl round her shoulders

Nelly Ah, there were two of us working here then. (*She sees Kesiah*) Here's Kesiah, ma'am.
Margaret Ah, Kesiah . . .
Kesiah Did you want me, Mrs Sumner?
Margaret Why yes, I did.
Nelly I'll just get some more logs.

Nelly brushes past Kesiah and exits through the kitchen

Kesiah You've something to tell me. Something on your mind.
Margaret Nothing very much. I just thought I ought to tell you that I asked that Miss Walsh to look in again this morning.
Kesiah Then where did she stay last night?
Margaret At *The Crown*. I shall pay her bill, of course.
Kesiah I see. It looks as if you've made up your mind.
Margaret By no means. But it seemed to me that Miss Walsh had possibilities. At least, she's better than the last applicant.
Kesiah You're not paying this Miss Walsh much of a compliment, considering the last one was half-witted, had only one eye and trouble with her breathing. Anyway, she looks more like a lady's maid than a housekeeper.
Margaret She might improve on further acquaintance. I'm thinking of you as well as myself. You don't want to spend the rest of your life here, do you?
Kesiah No no. Of course I don't. (*But the tone belies her words*) It's just that I'd like to be sure you're properly suited.
Margaret That's most kind of you, Kesiah.

Nelly enters from the kitchen

Nelly Doctor Graham is just coming down the lane.
Margaret (*agitated*) She mustn't see me like this. (*To Kesiah*) Keep her talking until I've tidied myself . . .

Margaret hurries from the room

Smiling, Kesiah looks after her

Kesiah As if the doctor cares how she looks.

Nelly Still, it gives you a chance to talk to the doctor, doesn't it?

Kesiah What do you mean?

Nelly Ah, you enjoy a chat with Doctor Graham. I've watched you at it. You get all grand and on your best behaviour.

Kesiah It's a nice change to talk to Doctor Graham—to converse with an educated person after spending so much of my time with an ignorant girl.

Nelly You do go on about your education. Pity you didn't make better use of it.

Kesiah seems about to reply; Nelly waves her to silence

All right! All right! Now I'll get the linen ready for the wash before you find me something else to do.

Nelly hurries out. Kesiah scowls after her but switches on an ingratiating smile as Doctor Helen Graham comes in. She is one of the early women practitioners and she is dressed with some severity in heavy tweeds. In her hand she carries the traditional doctor's black bag. She is about the same age as Kesiah

Kesiah Ah, Doctor. It's good to see you. We never see a soul here.

Dr Graham Still here then, Kesiah? I thought you'd have been on your way by now.

Kesiah I'm in no hurry.

Dr Graham No more applicants for the post of housekeeper? (*She places her bag on the table*)

Kesiah There's one coming this morning but I don't think she'll suit.

Dr Graham You'd better let me find somebody for you.

Kesiah You'd be doing me a bad turn if you did.

Dr Graham Where's Mrs Sumner?

Kesiah In her room. She asked you to give her a few minutes. Will you take a glass of sherry wine, Doctor?

Dr Graham Thank you, yes.

Kesiah Please sit down.

Dr Graham sits on one of the chairs at the table. Kesiah goes to the cupboard and takes out bottle and glasses. The Doctor surveys the room critically. Kesiah brings bottle and glasses to the table

Dr Graham I should have thought this place would have been too lonely for you.

Kesiah (*pouring the drinks*) I've been lonelier. (*She gives the Doctor her sherry*) I've also been colder and hungrier.

Dr Graham So you're prepared to stay?

Kesiah Until the spring—if it can be managed.

Dr Graham We'll have to arrange it.

Dr Graham raises her glass. Kesiah does likewise

Here's success, Kesiah. But I'm surprised you want to stay. It can't be exactly—cosy here.

Kesiah It isn't, but I have food, warmth and a bed. I'm enjoying the luxury of not being an outcast. You don't know what it means to be an outcast.

Dr Graham That's where you're wrong. I'm a freak—a woman doctor. I'm only tolerated because I'm partner to my father.

Kesiah I'm sure that's not true.

Dr Graham Oh, but it is. The patients say: "Of course she learned a lot from her father." The truth is that I'm twice the doctor he is but nobody will acknowledge the fact. Women doctors will be accepted at their true worth but not in my time. So you see I'm an outcast, too. (*She sighs and drinks*) Anyway, I hope you stay—this other woman might not be so hospitable.

Kesiah And she wouldn't want to stay—not if she saw Mrs Sumner in one of her bouts.

Dr Graham We'll have a word about that before I go. She's drinking because she's worried about her niece. If she could only hear from her, there would be an immediate improvement.

Kesiah I can't understand it. Some days Mrs Sumner writes two long letters to her. I know because I post them myself. Why doesn't the girl reply?

Dr Graham There was a bitter quarrel before she left. Perhaps she doesn't want to make it up.

Kesiah Not when she learns that her aunt is ill and troubled? She couldn't be so heartless!

Dr Graham Then the letters aren't being forwarded. I suppose it's difficult to trace a touring actress. (*She finishes her drink*) I'd better go and see Mrs Sumner. Thank you, Kesiah.

Kesiah rises in anticipation. Dr Graham rises and hands Kesiah her glass

I hope you're still here next time I come.

Dr Graham exits

Kesiah stands gazing thoughtfully into the empty glass. Then, hearing a sound, she swiftly gathers up the bottle and glasses and returns them to the cupboard

Nelly comes in carrying a clothes basket filled with soiled linen

Nelly There you are—I timed it nicely.

Kesiah What do you mean, girl?

Nelly I met the doctor on the stairs. Did you have a nice conversation between educated people?

Kesiah I don't see that it has anything to do with you. As a matter of fact, Doctor Graham wished to have a word with me about Mrs Sumner's illness.

Nelly Did she now? She ought to tell her to leave the bottle alone. Then other people would be able to sleep at night instead of listening to her screaming when she gets the horrors.

Kesiah (*sharply*) You're getting above yourself, Nelly! You're not to say such things about your mistress!

Nelly You should talk! You say worse than that.

Kesiah I do nothing of the kind

Nelly Yes you do—to her face sometimes. But you take good care that she's too drunk to understand what you're saying. (*She turns to go outside but, struck by a recollection, she pauses*) Did you give her the letter? It might be the one she's waiting for.

Kesiah What letter?

Nelly The one the postman gave you. The one that came this morning.

Kesiah That was for me.

Nelly (*contemptuous*) For you? Who'd write to you?

Kesiah All sorts of people. This was about my daughter.

Nelly The one you can't abide?

Kesiah I have only the one daughter.

Nelly And from what you told me, she'd never write to you.

Kesiah I never said she had written. I said the letter was *about* my daughter. It seems she's in trouble. The friend who wrote thought I should know.

Nelly (*still not wholly convinced*) I see. I don't care who writes to you. Only I thought that letter was for Mrs Sumner.

Nelly goes out

Kesiah stares balefully after her

Kesiah You'll have to go, my girl. You'll have to go very soon. I can't have you here. (*From her apron pocket, she takes an unopened letter and takes a quick, confirmatory glance through the window to establish Nelly's whereabouts. Doubtfully, she studies the address on the envelope, turns it over and then returns it to her pocket. She looks reflectively about the room and her face lights up when she sees the purse on the dresser. Swiftly, she goes over to the dresser, picks up the purse and weighs it in her hand. She smiles as if the purse held the key to relieve her present difficulties. As she hears somebody coming, she hastily slips the purse in her apron pocket*)

Dr Graham comes in; her expression is grave

Dr Graham Kesiah, I have just examined Mrs Sumner and I find her much worse since my last examination.

Kesiah I'm sorry to hear that.

Dr Graham It's her heart. (*She puts down her bag and sits on one of the chairs at the table*) She's got to rest more and drink less. She's apparently had one attack recently and it's weakened her. I'm going to ask you to see that she takes less drink and spends more time in bed.

Kesiah You can rely on me, Doctor.

Dr Graham If she doesn't behave, I'll have to take steps.

Kesiah What would they be, Doctor?

Dr Graham As she refuses to go into hospital, I would have to bring in a
trained nurse.

Kesiah That won't be necessary. I understand her. I can look after her.

Dr Graham I'm sure you'll do your best. (*She rises, picks up her bag, places
it on the table and opens it*) Here are some pills. (*She takes a small box
from the bag and gives it to Kesiah*) I've given Mrs Sumner a box but you
keep this as an added precaution. If she has any further attacks, she must
take two of these in water. You understand?

Kesiah Yes. It's serious then, Doctor.

Dr Graham Quite serious. I wish we could get in touch with the niece. I'll
look in each day now. But send for me immediately if she has an attack.
(*She closes her bag and prepares for departure*) Good morning, Kesiah.

Kesiah Good morning, Doctor.

Dr Graham goes out

*Kesiah goes to the window and watches her departure. She thrusts the box of
pills into the pocket of her apron. As she does so, her hand encounters an un-
familiar object which she brings forth. It is Margaret's purse. Recollection
flares in her face. She looks round cautiously and closes the door. She opens
the purse and takes from it three sovereigns. With these in her hand, she
crosses to the coat hooks and thrusts the three coins into the pocket of Nelly's
coat. She replaces the purse in its original position on the dresser and opens
the door. She hears Margaret approaching and goes over to the window*

Margaret enters; she looks dejected

Kesiah The doctor's just going, ma'am.

Margaret (*not interested*) Is she? (*After a pause*) It seems I'm a sick woman,
Kesiah.

Kesiah I'm sorry to hear that, Mrs Sumner. Very sorry indeed.

Margaret Doctor Graham says I'm to avoid excitement and . . . alcohol.
And I'm to rest more. (*She crosses to the armchair and she sits. An expression of grief clouds her face*) I may not be here when Clare gets back—I
could be dead before she gets here.

Kesiah You've done your best. Nobody could do more than you have.
You've written to her, been to look for her and still she makes no sign.
She's a cruel unnatural girl!

Margaret She's nothing of the sort! I won't allow you to say a word
against her. It was my fault. (*In a different tone as she turns away*) I said
unforgivable things to her before she left. Unforgettable things . . .

Kesiah But if she knows you're ill . . .

Margaret (*wearily*) I've told her. I've told her repeatedly in my letters.

Kesiah (*indignantly*) Then I say again, she's a cruel, unnatural girl!

Margaret (*rising*) You're not to say such things? Who are you to criticise
your betters? You would do well to remember your place, gipsy! (*She
glares angrily at Kesiah*)

Kesiah I'm sorry. (*She is suddenly very humble*) Please forgive me. I was always one to speak my mind. (*Remembering*) You were going to give me money to pay the baker's roundsman.

Margaret So I was. I left my purse in here. Now where . . . (*She looks around in search of it, sees it on the dresser and goes to pick it up. She opens the purse, looks within and raises her head incredulously*) Kesiah . . .

Kesiah Yes?

Margaret Where's the money that was in my purse? There are three sovereigns missing.

Kesiah I don't know where they are—it's no good looking at me like that. (*Her expression brightens as if she has suddenly recollected something significant*) Wait a minute. Wait a minute. Perhaps I do know . . .

Margaret (*sarcastically*) I'm sure you do. Just give yourself time.

Kesiah No, no. It was that girl. (*She waves her hand in the direction of the door*) I'm sure of it. She was over there. Just a minute—I'll call her. (*She hurries into the kitchen and then we hear her calling from the open door*) Nelly! Nelly! Come here! (*She comes back to Margaret*)

Margaret I think you're mistaken. She's never taken anything from here.

Kesiah Maybe not. But there's always a first time. I tell you I saw her.

Nelly comes in drying her hands on her apron

Nelly (*as she comes in*) Now what is it? I'll never get the washing done at this rate. (*Suddenly conscious of the atmosphere, she pauses and looks from one to the other*) What's the matter?

Kesiah (*belligerently*) Where is it? Where's the money you took from Mrs Sumner's purse?

Nelly Me? I never took it. I never took anything in my life!

Kesiah We'll see. We'll see about that. (*She closes the door. The coat hooks are now in full view*) Mrs Sumner . . .

Margaret Yes?

Kesiah Would you look in the pocket of the coat (*pointing*) hanging over there?

Margaret looks bewildered and does not move

Please. It's better that you should.

Margaret goes towards the coat hooks

Go on, Mrs Sumner. Try the pockets.

Nelly Try where you like. You won't find anything.

But, from Margaret's expression, it is clear that she has found something. She withdraws her hand and shows three shining coins on the palm of her hand. Nelly looks from Margaret's extended hand to her face in shocked disbelief

Nelly I never took the money! I don't know how it got there!

Margaret Of course you took it! How else did it get there?

Nelly (*glancing at Kesiah*) I think I could guess.
Margaret So you're accusing Kesiah? Why should she put my money in your pocket?

Margaret raises her hand as Nelly is about to reply

Don't answer. Impudence is one thing. Dishonesty is another. I won't have it. Oh!

Margaret grimaces with pain. Immediately, Kesiah is beside her and has thrown a supporting arm around her

Kesiah You're exciting yourself. Remember what the doctor said. I'll see to this.
Margaret All right. I'll go and lie down for a little while. (*She frees herself from Kesiah, starts for the door but turns again*) See that she's gone before I come downstairs again.

Kesiah opens the door

Margaret, holding her side, goes out slowly

Kesiah You heard what Mrs Sumner said.
Nelly I heard. Well, you managed it.
Kesiah Managed what?
Nelly You've been trying to get rid of me ever since you came. I hope you're satisfied.
Kesiah You'd better go or I'll send for the police.
Nelly I'll go—I know you wouldn't want the police here.

Ellen Walsh enters

Kesiah You're not doing yourself any good, my girl. If you're not on your way . . . (*She breaks off*)

Ellen stands looking embarrassed because she has clearly intruded on a heated altercation. She is exceedingly neat, very prim, most refined and quite correct. She is in her forties and her immaculate appearance contrasts sharply with the sordid room and its other occupants

Ellen I'm so sorry if I intrude but I did knock. Twice, in fact.
Kesiah It's quite all right, Miss Walsh. I shall be with you in just a moment. If you wouldn't mind sitting over there . . .

Kesiah indicates the chairs over by the table and, keeping an apprehensive eye on Nelly while giving her the widest possible berth, Ellen steers her way over and sits down. She continues to observe Nelly fearfully

This—this person is just about to leave.

Nelly And that's the truth for once. (*She takes her coat from its hook and struggles into it*) What about my wages?

Kesiah (*with great dignity*) If Mrs Sumner decides that anything is due to you, she'll see you get it.

Nelly Fat chance of that with you around. (*She starts towards the door but turns to deliver a Parthian shot*) I'm certainly glad to see the last of you!

Nelly rushes from the room

Kesiah (*calling after her*) Not nearly as glad as I am to see the back of you! (*Switching abruptly from the strident to the near-dulcet, she turns to Ellen*) You must have received a very bad impression of us here, Miss Walsh, but there have been strange happenings here this morning.

Ellen Indeed?

Kesiah It has been necessary to get rid of that girl. However, let us hope it won't be too difficult to replace her. Girls just won't come here—not even for double wages.

Ellen And why is that?

Kesiah Well—I find this rather difficult. (*She hesitates*) Didn't they tell you anything at *The Crown*?

Ellen remains silent

Anything about Mrs Sumner?

Ellen They said she was eccentric.

Kesiah And that was all? (*She sits in the chair opposite Ellen*)

Ellen (*reluctantly*) Er—no. They said she drank. But I don't pay any attention to gossip.

Kesiah You would do well to do so on this occasion. Why do you think we had to get rid of that girl in such a hurry?

Ellen I have no idea. Why did you?

Kesiah (*darkly*) I'd prefer you to find out for yourself.

Ellen She does drink then? Mrs Sumner, I mean?

Kesiah Heavily. The doctor was here this morning and warned her about her drinking but it won't have any effect. It wouldn't be so bad if she became quietly intoxicated.

Ellen But she doesn't?

Kesiah No. The trouble is she gets violent. However, I'm sure you'll be able to deal with her.

Ellen I'm far from sure—I have no experience of such a situation. Besides, I'm a delicate woman. You never know where you are when the mistress drinks.

Kesiah Then there's the loneliness.

Ellen Yes, I suppose it is lonely here.

Kesiah Lonely! A week here seems like an age. Nowhere to go on your evening off. You'd be cooped up day and night with her—week after week—month after month—year after year.

Ellen (*smiling uncertainly*) But we'd be all right. We'd get on well together. I can tell that at once.

Kesiah Oh, I won't be here ten minutes after you've come.
Ellen No?
Kesiah (*whispering hoarsely*) I want to be away before dark.
Ellen (*intimidated*) Why before dark?
Kesiah Because I've had enough of the ghost.
Ellen Ghost? What ghost?
Kesiah The ghost of Janey Johnson.
Ellen (*with an attempt at firmness*) I don't believe in ghosts.
Kesiah That's all right then.

There is a brief silence during which Kesiah watches the visitor narrowly. It is obvious that Ellen is very frightened

Ellen (*swallowing*) Who—who was Janey Johnson?
Kesiah The previous housekeeper.
Ellen What happened to her?
Kesiah She was sent to get wine from the cellar for Mrs Sumner and she fell down the cellar steps. Some say she was pushed . . .
Ellen Who is supposed to have pushed her?
Kesiah (*after a careful glance to left and right*) That I leave you to discover. (*She rises and points*) That's the cellar door. You hear Janey moaning at the bottom of the steps. But that's not the worst.
Ellen No?
Kesiah (*advancing stealthily on Ellen*) She shrieks as she starts to come up the stairs.

Ellen shrinks away

I've never waited to see if she comes into the kitchen. But it's more than flesh and blood can stand. I haven't slept a wink for three nights. (*She takes the keys from her belt and thrusts them into Ellen's hand*) Here, take these. I'm glad to be rid of them.
Ellen But I haven't said that I'd . . .
Kesiah I've had enough of this place and of Mrs Sumner. I'm off. It's your turn now.

Ellen makes a half-hearted attempt to rise; Kesiah waves her back

Stay where you are. Don't move.

Ellen subsides

Ellen Where are you going?
Kesiah To tell Mrs Sumner you're here.

Kesiah hurries from the room

Ellen rises and calls after her

Ellen Come back, please! Come back!

Kesiah either does not hear or ignores her. Ellen surveys the room with min-

gled fear and disgust. Her roving glance comes to rest on the cellar door and she goes over to it. Greatly daring, she opens it and peers within. She jumps at an imagined noise, and hastily closes the door

> *Ellen flees from the room. A moment later she is back again—she still has the keys in her hand, but rids herself of them by throwing them on the table before running out of the room even faster than before.*
> *The room is empty for a moment, and then Kesiah returns*

Smiling, Kesiah picks up the bunch of keys and restores them to her belt. Then she goes to the window and laughs softly as she watches the later stages of Ellen's departure

Kesiah That's another one I don't have to bother about.

Margaret, looking worn and dispirited, comes in

Kesiah turns. Margaret goes to the armchair and sits listlessly

Margaret I can't get used to it, Kesiah. I just can't get used to regarding myself as an invalid.

Kesiah You'll have to take care. You've been neglecting yourself.

Margaret I thought I heard voices. Shouldn't Miss Walsh be here by now?

Kesiah She's been. She didn't stay very long.

Margaret You mean she's gone?

Kesiah That's right. Gone and not coming back. She's like all the rest—she took one look at this place and ran off as fast as her legs could carry her. You'll never get anybody to stay here.

Margaret But I had such hopes of her.

Kesiah Oh, had you? I've had about enough, too. It's time I went.

Margaret *(troubled)* Going, Kesiah? What shall I do if you go?

Kesiah I don't know. But I've been here too long for my own good. I was only to stay until the new housekeeper came. According to our arrangement, there's a matter of five pounds due to me.

Margaret *(rising and going to her)* But you can't—you can't go.

Kesiah I don't see what's to keep me. I'm not doing any good here.

Margaret But you are. You're bearing me company through these dreadful days and nights. I feel safer with you here. *(Putting a hand on her arm)* Please stay, Kesiah. It may not be for long.

Kesiah *(turning away)* That's why I ought to go now. If anything happened to you, your niece would come here and turn me out. I would have served my purpose.

Margaret I'll alter my will. I'll leave things so that she will have to provide you with a home.

Kesiah And lock us up here like two prisoners in the same cell? From what I've heard of her, I wouldn't care to live in her house. We'd hate one another! No, that wouldn't serve!

Margaret What shall I do then? What can I do to make you stay?

Kesiah *(regarding her steadily)* You could leave the house to me.

There is a silence during which Margaret gently shakes her head

Margaret No. No, I couldn't do that. I couldn't take this house away
  from my sister's child.
Kesiah Couldn't you? That's most forgiving and considerate of you! What
  has she done to deserve it? Is she here to nurse and comfort you? Does
  she reply to your letters?

Margaret is silent

  Answer me. You owe me an answer.
Margaret No, Kesiah. She doesn't reply to my letters.
Kesiah Does her conduct show affection? Would you say that she is fond
  of you when she can let you worry your heart out for want of a line or
  two from her?
Margaret I told you, Kesiah, that the fault was mine. I was beside myself
  when she went away. I said things not easily forgiven.
Kesiah But you've apologized. You've begged her to write to you.
Margaret (*suddenly suspicious*) How do you know?
Kesiah (*taken aback*) You—you told me.
Margaret (*vaguely, as she brushes her hand across her face*) I don't
  remember.
Kesiah It was—it was when you'd had a few drinks the other night.
Margaret I drink too much and then I talk foolishly. I must take hold of
  myself. The doctor said I mustn't drink.

Kesiah moves purposefully towards the door

  Where are you going?
Kesiah Upstairs. To get my bits and pieces together.
Margaret (*distressed*) Oh, no! No, Kesiah!
Kesiah Why should I stay here? Tell me that! To keep the place ready for
  your niece when she chooses to come? Not me! Not Kesiah! I won't
  benefit a creature who can be so callous and vindictive!
Margaret (*following her*) Kesiah, I beseech you! (*She halts Kesiah by
  getting between her and the door*) Don't, for God's sake, leave me here
  alone!
Kesiah (*unmoved*) If you'll have my money ready for me when I come
  down . . .
Margaret But you said you'd wait until I got a new housekeeper. (*She puts
  a detaining hand on Kesiah's arm*) I still haven't got one.
Kesiah Very well. (*Firmly, she removes the restraining hand*) If you think
  I haven't earned my money, I'll go without it.

*Kesiah moves again in the direction of the door. As she reaches it, Margaret
shrieks*

Margaret Kesiah!

Kesiah turns. She senses victory as she recognises the authentic note of surrender

Kesiah Yes?

Margaret I'll do it. I'll change my will. The solicitor can come out to-morrow.

Kesiah And you won't go back on your word?

Margaret No. I'll do as you ask. I couldn't live here alone. Perhaps die here alone . . .

Kesiah You shouldn't talk like that. Go and lie down for a while—you'll feel better when you've had a rest.

Margaret trails miserably to the door, where she pauses

Margaret You wouldn't call Clare callous and vindictive, Kesiah, if you'd known her. She was good—and gay—and kind. So very kind.

Margaret leaves the room

Kesiah waits for a moment before she stalks to the kitchen door, where she looks off to ensure that Margaret has indeed gone. As she walks over to the armchair, she takes the letter from her apron pocket. She tears open the envelope and proceeds to read it. As she reaches the end of the letter, she quotes

Kesiah "Your heartbroken Clare". (*She rises, goes to the fireplace, and throws the letter and envelope into the fire. She smiles as she watches them burn*) You'd be more heartbroken still, Clare, if you knew that you'd just lost your inheritance to a gipsy.

Curtain

ACT II

SCENE 1

The same. A few days later, evening

It is dark outside. When the CURTAIN *rises, Kesiah and her visitor, Rose
Farnley, are sitting at the table. They are drinking, and it is reasonably safe to
presume that they are drinking gin because there is a bottle of that spirit on
the table. Rose is a slatternly, ageing woman whose main interests in life are
drink and gossip—in that order. Kesiah's expression suggests that her guest
is in some danger of outstaying her welcome*

Rose And isn't it lucky that I happened to find myself near your back door
when the storm broke?

Kesiah Very lucky. Especially considering that the storm got you a drink.

Rose Yes, indeed. (*She holds her drink at arm's length and studies it critically*) I was always one to be thankful for small mercies. (*She sips and
regards Kesiah quizzically*)

Kesiah (*half rising*) Are you suggesting . . .

Rose (*waving her down*) Not for a moment. Not for a single, solitary
moment. I'm sure it is very kind of you to ask me in out of the storm and
more than kind of you to dispense your open-handed hospitality to an
old woman who (*raising her glass*) —wishes you well. (*She sips again*)

Kesiah Here, give me your glass. (*She rises, picks up the bottle and removes
the cork*)

Rose No, no. There's no need. (*Unconvincingly, she covers the top of her
glass with her hand*)

Kesiah (*determined*) Give me your glass.

*Rose downs the remainder of her drink with a speed born of long practice and
then holds out her glass expectantly. Kesiah fills it almost to the brim and
Rose registers appreciation. As an afterthought, Kesiah tops up her own glass*

Kesiah Is that to your liking, Mrs Farnley?

Rose Very much so. (*Confidentially*) I need gin for my complaint.

Kesiah And what is your complaint?

Rose Thirst.

*Rose laughs loudly and wheezily, but breaks off when she sees that Kesiah is
regarding her stonily*

And don't call me Mrs Farnley. Call me Rose.

Kesiah Rose?

Rose That's my name. My poor husband—rest his soul!—used to say:

"You're rightly named Rose. You are the loveliest flower of them all."
(*She preens herself*) That's what he used to say.

Kesiah I take it he has been dead for some time.

Rose He has indeed. It's thirty years since I lost him. Thirty years this coming December.

Kesiah (*nodding*) I see.

Rose You've got a sympathetic nature, Kesiah. You don't mind if I call you Kesiah?

Kesiah Most people do whether I like it or not.

Rose Yes, you've got a sympathetic nature. Anybody can see that. Because you've known trouble. (*She sighs*) You can always tell—I knew we'd become good friends from the moment we met in the four-ale bar of *The Crown*.

Kesiah Just a moment. I don't recall that we actually met.

Rose Well—not—not formally.

Kesiah As I remember it, you came up to me and asked me to buy you a drink.

Rose That's right. As I said, it was all informal at the time.

Kesiah Then you asked me to buy you another drink and after that you said you'd buy me one but you'd left your purse at home.

Rose (*with an embarrassed smile*) Fancy you remembering that.

Kesiah Oh, I recollect that evening very well. It was the only time I've been out since I came here.

Rose Very lonely you must find it in this place, Kesiah—just you and Mrs Sumner.

Kesiah Yes, I went up to the bar and the barman—and the barman . . . (*She snaps her fingers in exasperation*) What's his name?

Rose Fred. Fred Betteridge. Been at *The Crown* for donkey's years.

Kesiah He said to me: "You watch out for her. She'll get you to buy a drink and when it's her turn, she'll tell you she's left her purse at home." And he was right, wasn't he?

Rose The cheek of him! Wait till I see him! That's defamation of character, that's what it is.

Kesiah And that wasn't all.

Rose No?

Kesiah He said: "She's been coming in here for as long as I remember and I've never yet seen her with a purse."

Rose He said that? He dared to say that?

Kesiah He also added something to the effect that the oldest living customer had never seen you with a purse.

Rose gasps—too horrified to speak

But he did say you possessed one outstanding recommendation.

Rose Oh, he did, did he? And what, pray, was that?

Kesiah He said you could drink any given quantity of liquor.

Rose (*sorrowfully shaking her head*) You shouldn't have listened to him, Kesiah. Everybody knows that Fred Betteridge is a born liar and troublemaker.

Kesiah It wasn't just him. Others said much the same thing.

Rose What others?

Kesiah There was the old woman in the black hat—the one who sat near the fire.

Rose Bridget Reilly. What had she to say?

Kesiah She described you as a sponge and a soak.

Rose (*indignantly*) She should talk! That Bridget Reilly has drunk more gin than there's water in the Irish Sea. She's jealous of me! They're all of them jealous of me!

Kesiah Why should they be jealous?

Rose Because I'm so popular. (*Impressively*) I am, without any doubt, the most popular person in the four-ale bar of *The Crown*.

Kesiah How on earth can you be popular when they all speak ill of you?

Rose Never mind about them. They're trash—every one of them. I am *very* well liked by—by—(*she falters and then finishes on a burst of inspiration*) by all those who like me.

Kesiah (*nodding gravely*) And I'm sure that's true.

Rose True as Gospel. It's enough to destroy one's faith in human nature. (*She reflects sadly*) When I think of all the custom I've brought to *The Crown* . . .

Kesiah You know what I would do in your place?

Rose What?

Kesiah I would consider transferring my patronage elsewhere.

Rose And I'd do it—I'd do it like a shot except . . .

Kesiah Yes?

Rose There isn't another pub within three miles.

Kesiah observes that Rose's glass is empty and, rising, she picks up the bottle

Kesiah Here, let me . . .

Rose rises and fiercely withdraws her glass

Rose No, no. You think I'm a —what was it?—a soak and a sponge.

Kesiah Of course I don't. You don't think I'd agree with them?

Rose You sounded as if you did.

Kesiah Just now you called them trash. (*Menacingly*) You don't think I'm trash, do you?

Rose No, no. Not for a moment. You're a kind soul, a generous soul, and —(*as if doing a favour*)—I'll have a drink with you.

Rose offers her glass and Kesiah fills it. Rose sits again and Kesiah follows her example

Rose How's Mrs Sumner?

Kesiah Not very well. She has heart trouble.

Rose So I hear—and that's not all I hear. (*She glances carefully around and then goes on hoarsely*) I'm told she's taken to the bottle.

Kesiah That is something upon which I cannot comment.

Rose (*warmly*) Just what I would expect from you. You are loyal, Kesiah, as well as generous. (*She drinks reflectively*) Ah, drink is a great comfort when used in moderation. But it's a terrible thing when it gets a grip of you.

Kesiah I'm sure you're right.

Rose Oh, yes. I know of some terrible cases—Bridget Reilly for one. Give Mrs Sumner my best wishes—my kindest regards.

Kesiah Do you know her?

Rose (*hesitantly*) Not exactly. Not to speak to . . . (*Brightly*) But I've seen her about from time to time.

Kesiah Then you could hardly build a lasting acquaintance on that foundation.

Rose No. But I have my feelings the same as anybody else and she has my sympathy. If she's as ill as all that shouldn't her niece be sent for?

Kesiah Niece? What niece?

Rose The one who used to live here. They were very close, I understand. Devoted to each other—so they said.

Kesiah Then all I can say is that the niece must have changed—and for the worse. She doesn't reply to Mrs Sumner's letters.

Rose Perhaps the letters aren't reaching her. (*She considers*) You could go to the police.

Kesiah (*rising*) The police? Whatever for?

Rose They sometimes find people who've gone missing.

Kesiah I don't think that Mrs Sumner would care to involve the police. (*She goes over to the window and looks out*) The rain's stopped.

Rose But it'll still be dark outside and wet underfoot.

Kesiah You'll have to go sometime—you can't stay here all night.

Rose rises and drains her glass

Rose I see. You want me to go.

Kesiah I don't wish to hurry you but I was thinking that your friends in *The Crown* will be wondering what has happened to you.

Rose It would do them no harm to wonder just for once in a while.

There is a brief awkward silence—more trying to Rose than Kesiah

Still, I suppose you've things to do.

Kesiah I've a great deal to do before I seek my bed tonight.

Rose Then I'll be on my . . . (*She sees Margaret and her voice trails off*)

Margaret enters slowly and painfully, with her hand pressed to her breast. Once inside the room she halts and stands staring before her, quite unaware of Rose's presence

Margaret I've got my pain, Kesiah. It's worse than ever. I can hardly get my breath.

Rose remains rooted to the spot watching Margaret with something between fear and fascination. Kesiah goes to her employer and puts a supporting arm around her

Kesiah Here, lean on me.

Supporting Margaret, Kesiah leads her to the armchair and eases her into it

Have you taken one of your pills?
Margaret As soon as the attack started but it's done no good. The pain is as bad as ever. (*She winces*) Worse, if anything.

Margaret closes her eyes. Kesiah regards her briefly and then turns to Rose

Kesiah You can see that she's very ill.
Rose (*nodding*) Oh, yes. I can see that—very ill. The poor woman!
Kesiah We need the doctor. I want you to go for her.
Rose It's too far—all that way in the wet and the cold. (*Plaintively*) And I'm not a well woman. (*She peers at Margaret*) Besides, she might be too late from the look of her.
Kesiah Late or not, we must have the doctor. Listen to me.

Rose is still staring fixedly at Margaret. Angrily, Kesiah shakes her

Listen to me carefully. Go as quickly as you can to the Beresford farm and tell Mr Beresford that Mrs Sumner has had an attack—is very ill. Ask him to telephone Dr Graham at once. If she's at home, she'll come right away.
Rose Will Mr Beresford be able to telephone Dr Graham?
Kesiah Of course he will. The Beresfords are patients of Dr Graham. Do you understand what you have to do?
Rose Yes. Go to the Beresford farm. Tell Mr Beresford that Mrs Sumner is ill. Ask him to telephone Dr Graham.
Kesiah That's it. Get off with you—and make haste.

Rose goes out

After a glance at Margaret, Kesiah follows as far as the doorway and calls after her

There's a lantern by the sink. Take it with you.

Kesiah comes back into the room and looks speculatively at Margaret, who is still sitting with her eyes closed

I wonder—I wonder . . .

Still watching Margaret, Kesiah backs to the table, picks up one of the kitchen chairs and places it some little distance from the armchair. She sits, folds her arms and settles herself as if in expectation of a lengthy vigil. In a moment Margaret sighs and opens her eyes

Margaret Oh, Kesiah . . .

Kesiah Do you still have the pain?

Margaret Yes, it's still there. (*She looks about her questioningly*) I thought I heard voices.

Kesiah No. You heard one voice—Janey's.

Margaret Janey's? But she's . . .

Kesiah She's dead. But she's here or hereabouts. I haven't seen her yet but I know that, sooner or later, I will see her. Why does she linger here? Were you unkind to her?

Margaret No, never unkind. I treated her well always. She said so.

Kesiah Or is it because of you that she's here? Is it because she met her death on an errand of yours?

Margaret It wasn't. You know it wasn't. It had nothing to do with me.

Kesiah That's not what you told me the other night when I was putting you to bed. You said then that you sent her to her death.

Margaret I did?

Kesiah That's what you said.

Margaret (*shaking her head*) I no longer know the difference between true or false, waking and dreaming, day or night. (*Turning to Kesiah piteously*) I'm very ill, aren't I?

Kesiah If you are, you've brought it on yourself. You drink too much—that's your trouble.

Margaret I shall not drink any more, Kesiah. You may be sure of that.

Kesiah You've said so before and, an hour or two later, I've had to put you to bed.

Margaret I have been a great trouble to you and I am sorry for it. But could I ask you to do something else for me?

Kesiah What is it?

Margaret I would like a glass of water. When we spoke of drink just now, we were not, I think, discussing water. If you please, Kesiah . . .

Kesiah I'll get it.

Kesiah goes out to the kitchen

Margaret writhes in the chair as she is gripped by a paroxysm of pain

Kesiah returns with a glass of water. She goes to Margaret and supports her

Margaret, with some difficulty, swallows a little of the water and then leans back exhausted

Kesiah More?

Margaret (*weakly*) No, thank you.

Kesiah places the glass on the table, returns to her chair and sits

Kesiah You have been most fortunate in that you have had me to fetch and carry for you these past weeks.

Margaret That is true. I have been fortunate and I appreciate all you have done.

Kesiah (*as if she had not spoken*) Especially when you consider how you received me that first night I came to this house. What was it you said?

Margaret You must make allowances—I had been drinking. I was not myself.

Kesiah (*rising*) It comes back to me. (*Pointing*) You were standing there. (*Pointing again*) And I was sitting there at the table until you ordered me to my feet.

Margaret I've told you, Kesiah, that I was drunk at the time.

Kesiah But it was when you came back later that the courtesies began. Do you recall what you said to me—the stranger under your roof? Because I do. "Gipsies live on other folk's leavings: a dry crust begged at the back door, eggs filched from the farmer's hen coop, herbs cooked in a pot or, now and then, a stolen chicken or a snared rabbit." And you asked if all that wasn't so.

Margaret Please stop. I can't bear it.

Kesiah But I had to—I had to bear it. I had to stand there and hear you giving your views on gipsies. "Lazy to the backbone and false as Judas. They contaminate the ground under their feet. They rob those who befriend them." Then you said: "But I'll tell you something, gipsy: you won't rob me." Have I robbed you?

Margaret No, no. I was much at fault. But all this is best forgotten.

Kesiah Forgotten? You claimed to know all about gipsies. But I'll tell you something you didn't know. A gipsy never forgets an insult, never forgives an injury—and I've never forgiven you!

Margaret Then it's high time you did, Kesiah. Time you forgave and forgot for I haven't much time left. You must understand that I've had a hard life since my husband died.

Kesiah A hard life! You don't know what hard living is. You've always been sure of a roof over your head and three square meals a day.

Margaret There are other things besides food and shelter. Love and companionship I had in full measure and I was lost without them.

Kesiah I've had to live without them all my life.

Margaret Then I am sorry for you. I can count my blessings—I was blessed in my husband and blessed in Clare.

Kesiah Oh, I thought we'd get back to her. She's never far from your thoughts.

Margaret And she seems very close just now. If she was here, she would forgive me. I am assured of that.

Kesiah She was very dear to you, wasn't she?

Margaret Very dear. More like a daughter than a niece—which is why I missed her so when she left.

Kesiah turns from her and reflects for a moment. Then, having reached a decision, she faces Margaret again

Kesiah I'm tempted to do you a kindness—

Margaret Kindness?

Kesiah —though whether you will recognize it as such is another matter.

Margaret I don't understand you.

Kesiah You will. You will when I tell you that Clare did write to you. She wrote often. She wrote repeatedly.

Margaret Then how was it I didn't . . .

Kesiah Very simple. I met the postman each morning and I burned her letters as they came.

Margaret (*incredulously*) Burned her letters!

Kesiah Yes. Just as I burned the letters you wrote to her and which you gave me so trustingly to post for you.

Margaret Why? Why did you do this?

Kesiah You've had one reason—because of what you said on that first evening.

Margaret And the other reason?

Kesiah I wanted this house and I meant to get it. It's mine now—legally mine and your Clare is as homeless as once I was.

Margaret is terribly shaken. Watched by Kesiah, she sits staring bleakly ahead as she tries to absorb the import of Kesiah's disclosure. Then she grips the arms of the chair and, summoning all her remaining strength, she thrusts herself up from the chair. She stands, uncertainly erect, supporting herself with one hand resting on the chair

Margaret Then I'll tell you something, gipsy, and remember this as well as all the rest: I know as I stand here that there is a God and I know just as certainly that He will not allow you to live here for very long. Make the most of it, gipsy!

The pain strikes Margaret again. She struggles for breath, wavers and slumps backwards into the chair. Momentarily, she is convulsed with pain and then, suddenly, she relaxes. Kesiah has watched unmoving. Now she goes to Margaret, stoops and listens for a heartbeat. Finding none, she registers relief. Still contemplating the body, she steps back

Kesiah For the rest of my life. For the rest of my natural life. That's how long I intend to live here. (*But it is evident from her voice and expression that she is considerably shaken and she retreats until she stands by the table. She sits, pours herself a drink from the gin bottle and looks again at Margaret*) And you were wrong when you said I hadn't robbed you—I robbed you of this house!

Kesiah drinks, as—

the CURTAIN falls

Scene 2

The same. Two weeks later, evening

Again it is dark outside. When the Curtain *rises Kesiah and Dr Graham are
sitting at the table, upon which are the elements of afternoon tea—cups and
saucers, plates, knives, teapot, cream jug and a cut cake. The atmosphere is
relaxed and friendly*

Kesiah More tea, Doctor? (*She feels the pot. The indications are that it is
cold*) I can easily make some fresh.

Dr Graham No, thank you. I never meant to stay as late as this but I've so
enjoyed our talk.

Kesiah I should have given you tea in the drawing room but it was just that
we got talking in here . . .

Dr Graham And quite right, too. It is most appropriate that we had tea
in here. After all, this is where we used to have our chats before you in-
herited. I'm very glad that you were left the house, Kesiah.

Kesiah Sometimes I think it is more than I deserve.

Dr Graham Not at all. You were Mrs Sumner's stay and support in her
last days, and she must have derived great comfort from your presence.
Will you be able to stay on here?

Kesiah Stay on here? Of course. That is, I mean to stay on. Why shouldn't
I?

Dr Graham I was thinking of the upkeep of this place—and the fact that
she left her money to the niece. You'll hardly be able . . .

Kesiah Oh yes, I will. Mr Beresford has made an offer for those fields
which march with his and some man from Rye is interested in the pad-
dock and the outbuildings.

Dr Graham Well, if you sell those . . .

Kesiah Then I should be able to sell what was the gardener's cottage. Of
course it has still to be arranged through the solicitors.

Dr Graham I'm glad to hear it. I was afraid that you might have to sell up
and move out. You've had no word from the niece?

Kesiah None—and I didn't expect any. Of course, not having her address,
I wasn't able to let her know of her aunt's death.

Dr Graham No. But I gather that Mrs Martell, the vicar's wife, heard from
her the week before Mrs Sumner died.

Kesiah (*disturbed*) Did she now?

Dr Graham Apparently they exchanged letters and Clare does know that
her aunt is dead.

Kesiah Then I suppose that, any time now, I can expect a visit from her.

Dr Graham Mrs Martell didn't think she would be coming this way for
quite some time. It seems she is on a theatrical tour of the North of
England.

Kesiah Best place for her.

Dr Graham Well. I really ought to be on my way. I have still to take
evening surgery.

She rises. So does Kesiah

Kesiah But don't let us forget the main purpose of your visit.
Dr Graham I'd honestly forgotten.
Kesiah (*going to the dresser*) Then it's lucky I remembered. (*She picks up two medium-sized parcels from the dresser and holds up the larger one*) That's the candlesticks and this—(*holding up the smaller parcel*)—is the coffee pot.
Dr Graham (*going to Kesiah and taking the parcels from her*) Thank you. I'll think twice before I admire anything else in a patient's house.
Kesiah Mrs Sumner wanted you to have them. She knew you'd give them a good home.
Dr Graham Silver has always been one of my weaknesses. If only it didn't tarnish so quickly.
Kesiah I've given those a good polishing today. It'll be some time before they need cleaning again. Could I give you a bag to put them in?
Dr Graham No, no. They'll be quite all right like this. I can manage them easily.

There is a knock at the back door

Kesiah Excuse me. I can't think who this can be . . .

Kesiah goes out through the kitchen and returns with Rose Farnley who is wearing a lugubrious expression

Rose Good evening, Doctor.
Dr Graham Good evening.
Rose I don't suppose you remember who I am.
Dr Graham Indeed I do. I have cause to remember you. You're Mrs Farnley and it was you who went to the Beresford farm and asked them to telephone me the night Mrs Sumner died.
Rose That I did. That I did, Doctor. But I knew then it was to no avail. I knew before I left this house there was nothing you could do for Mrs Sumner. I said: "The poor woman has death written all over her face." (*Turning to Kesiah*) Didn't I say that? Didn't I say that to you, Kesiah?
Kesiah (*bleakly*) Not that I recall.
Rose (*as if she had not spoken*) Mrs Sumner sat there in that—(*pointing to the armchair*)—chair and I stood—(*she moves to the precise spot and faces the armchair*)—here. I looked at her and I said to myself: "She's not long for this world."
Dr Graham You have, perhaps, some experience of nursing, Mrs Farnley?
Rose Not to speak of. But it didn't need experience of nursing to see that she wasn't long for here. I tell you it was written on her face. I stood here . . .
Dr Graham Yes, yes. You must excuse me. I have to get back for evening surgery.

Dr Graham starts for the kitchen with Kesiah following

Good night, Mrs Farnley.
Rose Good night, Doctor.
Kesiah (*as she goes out*) I won't be a moment.

Kesiah and Dr Graham go out

Left alone, Rose submits the room to a thorough survey, and takes note of the tea-things on the table

Having seen Dr Graham to the door, Kesiah returns. Her expression is the reverse of welcoming

Rose What was the doctor doing here?
Kesiah If you must know, she called to collect some small items left to her by Mrs Sumner. But, if you ask me, I'd say that was no business of yours. More to the point—what are you doing here?
Rose Oh, I came to congratulate you. I thought I would let a little time elapse and then I would come round to congratulate you—(*She is beginning to wilt before the intensity of Kesiah's hard, cold stare*)—on being left the house—and everything.
Kesiah I see. (*She goes to the far side of the table*) Perhaps you'll sit here at the table.

Kesiah indicates the chair opposite and, intimidated, Rose complies

Could I offer you a cup of tea?
Rose (*hesitantly*) Well, no, thank you. I find tea in the evenings very lowering.
Kesiah Do you now? Then I might as well get rid of these. (*She takes a tray from the dresser and places the tea things on it*) We'll have this table clear for a start. (*With the tray loaded, she pauses*) Could I get you something to eat?
Rose No, no. I'm not—hungry. (*The pause before the last word is clearly intentionally significant*)

Kesiah nods grimly, and bustles into the kitchen with the tray

Rose sits looking ill at ease

Kesiah returns and halts, hands on hips, surveying Rose

Kesiah I'm trying to decide why you walked all this way in the dark.
Rose (*her embarrassment increasing*) I told you. It was to congratulate you . . .
Kesiah Not you. I'd say you'd outworn your welcome at *The Crown* and

you thought there might be a drink or two and some easy pickings here. Am I right?

Rose (*offended*) They're always pleased to see me in *The Crown*.

Kesiah Then all I can say is that they're very good at concealing their pleasure. (*She relaxes her forbidding expression*) Would you like a drink?

Rose (*kindling immediately*) There's nothing I'd like better.

Kesiah goes to the cupboard, produces the gin bottle and glasses and brings them to the table. She sits and pours out two drinks watched appreciatively by Rose. Kesiah's gesture invites Rose to take one of the glasses which she does with alacrity raising it to Kesiah in almost the same movement

Your good health.

Kesiah And yours.

They drink and, when Kesiah speaks again, her tone is suddenly more friendly

What had you in mind when you stumbled along the muddy lanes? You surely had some purpose—some hope of benefit? (*Persuasively, as she leans forward*) Didn't you now?

Rose Well, I did. I won't attempt to deceive you.

Kesiah You couldn't if you tried.

Rose I did have a hope—that you might be inclined to share your good luck with me.

Kesiah Good luck? No luck about it. I was rewarded for my care of Mrs Sumner.

Rose Just the same, your circumstances have improved and people are very rarely rewarded in this world according to their deserts.

Kesiah How true. Your glass is empty. Let me, on this occasion at least reward you according to your deserts. (*She fills Rose's glass*)

Rose Thank you.

Kesiah This house was left to me but I shall have to go carefully to work if I am to find the money to maintain it and keep myself. So you see I am in no position . . .

Rose (*regarding her craftily*) Two women died in this house.

Kesiah (*immediately alert and very much on her guard*) What do you mean by that?

Rose Just this: between them they must have left a lot of clothes and bits and pieces you'd rather be without.

Kesiah And why would I rather be without them?

Rose (*assuming a sanctimonious expression*) Because they remind you, every time you see them, of those who are sadly departed.

Kesiah Neither Janey nor Mrs Sumner were kin to me so seeing their clothes about doesn't trouble me at all. What would you do if I gave them to you? Would you wear them? Or give them away?

Rose I wouldn't do either. There's a woman in Old Romsey will give me a good price for them.

Kesiah (*smiling*) Ah-h! Now I understand. Why shouldn't I sell the clothes to the woman myself?

Rose Because you don't need the money as badly as I do.

Kesiah That's a matter of opinion. (*She rises*) I'll tell you what I'll do.

Rose Yes?

Kesiah I'll give you some of the clothes and in return you tell me the name and address of this woman. Is it a deal?

Rose (*rising also*) Yes. Can I take the clothes now?

Kesiah Not now. I'll need to look them out. You call back in a day or two and I'll have them ready for you.

Rose Very well. Then I'll be on my way.

Rose finishes her drink and darts an eloquent glance at the bottle. Kesiah remains unmoved. Rose sighs and moves slowly towards the kitchen

Yes, I'll be on my way. (*She checks and then adds brightly*) But I'll be back.

Kesiah (*with no answering warmth*) There's nothing in this life more certain.

Shepherded by Kesiah, Rose exits to the kitchen

After a moment Kesiah returns, deep in thought. Morosely, she sits in the chair she recently vacated, and is just about to pour herself a drink when she pauses to listen intently

She sets down the bottle, rises, and fairly runs from the room

There is a moment or two of silence, and then Kesiah is heard speaking from the region of the back door

Kesiah (*off*) What were you doing there? Come here! Come inside! I want to look at you!

Kesiah comes in dragging by the wrist a struggling girl of indeterminate age—somewhere between the late teens and early twenties. Kesiah pulls her by the wrist and fairly shoves her into the middle of the room. The girl stands there—dirty, travel-stained and frightened as she rubs her arm and stares at Kesiah

The girl Don't hurt me, missus. Don't hurt me. I've done no harm.

The girl speaks with a country accent and in a rather laboured fashion which suggests that she is not very bright. Kesiah inspects her and the girl is increasingly intimidated

Kesiah What's your name?

The girl Please, it's Deborah.

Kesiah Deborah what?

Deborah Please, it's Deborah Barker.

Kesiah Where have you come from?

Deborah I've walked from Burmarsh since this morning.

Kesiah That's not very far.

Deborah I got lost twice, missus. And I haven't had a bite all day. Not all day, missus.

Kesiah Stay there. Don't move.

Kesiah goes into the kitchen

Deborah stares vacantly about her and continues to rub her arm

Kesiah comes in carrying a plate of bread and cheese in one hand and a beaker of milk in the other

Sit down. Over there.

Deborah sits at the table. Kesiah sets the food and drink in front of her. Deborah looks at her and does not touch the food until Kesiah says

Go on. Eat it.

Deborah begins to eat ravenously with Kesiah watching her dispassionately. Conscious of Kesiah's regard, Deborah glances at her

Deborah Thank you, missus.

Kesiah That's all right, girl. Where were you before you started to walk from Burmarsh?

Deborah Where? Until a week ago, I was in an orphanage. I was brought up there and they let me stay on to work for them when my time was up.

Kesiah That was kind of them.

Deborah Yes—wasn't it? Then they sent me to work in a private house.

Kesiah That was better, surely.

Deborah No, it wasn't. (*She drinks from the beaker and registers satisfaction*) Hey, this here is milk.

Kesiah Good for you. Why wasn't it better in the private house?

Deborah I didn't like it. The man was always following me about.

Kesiah Was he indeed? (*She sits opposite to Deborah prepared to be entertained by the girl's disclosures*)

Deborah That wasn't the worst of it.

Kesiah No?

Deborah He kept kissing me.

Kesiah (*pretending to be shocked*) Did he really?

Deborah Yes, he did. I didn't like it—his chin was all rough and bristly. One day his wife came in when he was kissing me. She didn't like it either. She beat me as if it was my fault. So I ran away.

Kesiah And quite right, too. So you're looking for another post?

Deborah I'm really looking for a home.

Kesiah (*laughing*) Are you then? Well, perhaps you've found one. I'm looking for a girl who's smart and willing.

Deborah (*eagerly*) Would I do, missus? I'm ever so willing (*Her face clouding over*) but they say I'm not very smart.

Kesiah Never mind, Deborah. Perhaps it's more important that you should be willing rather than smart. I wouldn't want anybody too smart around me.

Deborah I'd do my best, missus. I promise you I'd do my very best.

Kesiah Stand up, girl. Let me look at you.

Deborah rises. She looks awkward and self-conscious

Deborah I'm real strong, missus—stronger than I look.

Kesiah Turn around. (*As Deborah begins to pivot*) Slowly. Slowly, now.

Deborah (*rotating slowly*) I haven't a big appetite. I don't eat much.

Kesiah Can you scrub and wash?

Deborah I was the best scrubber and washer in the whole orphanage.

Kesiah You can stop turning now.

Deborah ceases to turn and faces Kesiah with a look of entreaty on her face

And can you bake and cook?

Deborah I can bake good bread and I can cook plain food without spoiling it.

Kesiah That's something, I suppose.

Kesiah considers while Deborah contemplates her anxiously. Kesiah, deep in thought, pours herself a drink. At length, she looks up

Yes. Yes, I think you might suit me.

Deborah registers relief

I'm inclined to give you a trial. (*She becomes aware of the glass in her hand and is recalled to a sense of hospitality. She flourishes her glass*) Would you like a drink?

Deborah (*recoiling*) Oh no, missus. Not me. I never touch it.

Kesiah (*laughing uproariously*) Better and better, Deborah. You're just the girl for me.

Deborah I hope so, missus.

Kesiah (*gravity restored*) Are you ready to make a start, girl?

Deborah Right away, missus. Right this very minute. But . . .

Kesiah (*displeased*) But what? Either you're ready or you're not.

Deborah I left my bundle outside. Can I bring it in?

Kesiah You can. Then come back here.

Deborah scurries from the room

Kesiah drinks reflectively

Deborah appears in the doorway carrying a dirty canvas bundle

Deborah Where shall I put it, missus?
Kesiah Leave it out there. Leave it in the kitchen.

Deborah withdraws momentarily. Then she rushes in and halts facing Kesiah

Deborah All ready, missus. All ready to begin.
Kesiah Good girl. Now listen to me—before you go to bed . . .
Deborah I haven't slept in a bed for three nights. Not for three nights have I slept in a bed.
Kesiah You shall tonight—when you've finished your work. I want you to go out into the kitchen. In the sink you'll find a pile of dirty dishes. There's a cloth on the side of the sink and there's hot water on the stove. Now what do you think I want you to do?

Deborah ponders and is briefly distressed. Then, light dawning, she smiles happily

Deborah You want me to wash those dishes.
Kesiah (*indulgently*) That's right. We'll soon learn to understand one another. Come back and tell me when you've done and I'll show you your room.
Deborah Right missus. (*She rushes out to the kitchen but returns almost at once*) Missus . . .
Kesiah Yes?
Deborah There's a right pile of dishes in that there sink.
Kesiah Too many? Are there too many for you?
Deborah Not for me. Never too many for me. I'll wash those dishes as good as new.
Kesiah Don't break any, mind.
Deborah I'll not break any. I'm that careful, missus. (*Going*) Don't you trouble yourself any more about those dishes.

Deborah exits to the kitchen

Kesiah (*smiling as she watches Deborah's departure*) I'll not trouble myself any more about them.

A clatter of dishes from the kitchen indicates that Deborah has begun operations

You're going up in the world, Kesiah. You're a lady with your own house and you've a maidservant to wait on you hand and foot. (*She sits basking in the glow of her improved situation*)

CURTAIN

SCENE 3

The same. Three days later, evening

It is again dark outside. When the CURTAIN *rises Kesiah is discovered sitting
at the table with the gin bottle and glass before her. She has been drinking—
but is not drunk—and she is somewhat dishevelled. In addition to the bottle
and glass there is a small handbell on the table. At first Kesiah is sunk in a
lethargy, but after a moment she rouses herself, picks up the bell and rings it
vigorously. She puts it down, but when there is no response to her ringing she
registers impatience. Again she shakes the bell, this time calling out*

Kesiah Deborah! Deborah!

*After a moment, Deborah enters breathlessly and stands, hands behind
her, facing her mistress in an attitude of respectful attention. If Kesiah is
dishevelled, Deborah redresses the balance for she is altogether much tidier
than when we saw her last. She is wearing a different dress, her hair is neatly
dressed and her whole appearance is neat and orderly in a scrubbed, institu-
tional fashion*

Deborah Yes, missus?
Kesiah Where have you been? You know that when I ring this bell (*And
she gives it a shake by way of demonstration*) I want you at once. (*Shouting*)
Where were you?
Deborah (*timidly*) Upstairs, missus. In your room.
Kesiah What were you doing there?
Deborah Making the bed.
Kesiah Making the bed! I've told you before, girl—the time for making
beds is in the morning.
Deborah (*defensively*) But I did make your bed this morning, missus. But
you went to lie down this afternoon. You were—you were tired. So I
was just making it again.
Kesiah (*contrite*) You're quite right, Deborah. I did go to bed this after-
noon and I *was* tired—didn't sleep at all well last night. You're a good
girl, Deborah.
Deborah (*embarrassed by the praise*) Thank you, missus.
Kesiah Yes, you are. (*She drinks*) And I've been bad tempered. But I've got
a lot on my mind—a great deal to worry me. I've got to sell this land and
these properties before I have money in the bank. When I have money, do
you know what I'll do?
Deborah No, missus.
Kesiah I'll start paying you wages.

Kesiah raises a hand to check Deborah's grateful reaction

Oh, not too much or you'll get ideas.
Deborah (*stolidly*) Not me, missus. I won't get no ideas.

Kesiah (*regarding her critically*) No, I don't suppose you will. Sit down a minute, Deborah.

Deborah sits in the opposite chair

Not many mistresses would ask their maids to sit down with them. You do realize that?

Deborah Yes, missus. You're very kind.

Kesiah And you know why? Because I remember when I had less than you have. Because I remember when I hadn't a crust to eat, hadn't a roof over my head and had scarcely a rag to my back. And me an educated woman who was brought up to be a lady. (*She empties her glass*)

Deborah Yes, you told me.

Kesiah (*sharply*) When? When did I tell you?

Deborah This afternoon—just before you went—you went to lie down.

Kesiah Oh, did I? H'm . . . (*She pours herself another drink and, with the bottle in her hand, smiles at Deborah*) Will you have a drink?

Deborah No, thank you, missus. I don't think it would suit me.

Kesiah (*putting down the bottle*) Nonsense—do you good. I'll get you to take a drink—you see if I don't. But I didn't tell you how I came by this house, did I?

Deborah shakes her head

I didn't tell you how I got it made over to me all legal and aboveboard . . .

Deborah You were going to tell me, missus, but then you came all over tired and sleepy-like.

Kesiah So I did. But I will tell you, Deborah. It will pass the time very pleasantly for us. You'll be interested. (*She drinks*) You'll be entertained. I came here one night by arrangement with Janey Johnson, the house-keeper. I was to stay here in comfort and rest for a few days.

Deborah That was nice for you, missus.

Kesiah Yes. But the arrangement was made when we believed the mistress would be away. When I got here, I found that she had returned un-expectedly.

Deborah What did she say?

Kesiah Told me that I wasn't welcome, gave me permission to stay the night and ordered me to be on my way next morning.

Deborah That wasn't kind. She was wicked.

Kesiah She was—and she paid for being wicked.

Deborah How? How did she pay?

Kesiah All in good time. She had to take her turn. First of all, I had to deal with the housekeeper. She was in the way. I had to get rid of her.

Deborah Get rid of her? I thought she was your friend.

Kesiah I had no friends. Janey Johnson only tolerated me because I used to read her hand. So what I did was to . . .

Both women are startled by sudden, loud knocking at the back door

Kesiah Who's that at this time of night? (*Then, recollecting*) Oh, yes! It'll be Rose Farnley. Go and let her in.
Deborah (*blankly*) Let her in? (*She sits unmoving*)
Kesiah (*impatiently*) Yes, let her in. Stir yourself.

Deborah still does not move

Come *on*, girl!

Deborah rises reluctantly and as reluctantly begins to move towards the kitchen

Here, wait a minute.

Deborah pauses

I don't really want to see her. There's a parcel of clothes out there in the kitchen. Give it to her and send her on her way.
Deborah Yes, missus.

As she turns to go, the knocking is repeated more loudly

Kesiah She's getting impatient. Come back when you've got rid of her.

Deborah goes

Kesiah listens, then shrugs, dismissing Rose, and drinks

Rose walks in, looking puzzled

Kesiah is startled

Rose Who's that? She opened the door and ran. Who is she?
Kesiah My maid.
Rose Maid? You've got a maid?
Kesiah I need somebody to do the rough work about the place.
Rose She wasn't here last time I came.
Kesiah No. I've only had her a day or two. She—er—came from an orphanage. I suppose you've come for the clothes.
Rose That's right. You said you'd look some out for me.
Kesiah I've been as good as my word. Would you like a drink?
Rose I wouldn't say "No".
Kesiah The day you do all the clocks will start to run backwards.
Rose (*hurt*) There's no need to make fun of my—little failing.
Kesiah Far be it from me . . . (*She rises with the intention of getting a glass for Rose but sways, totters and grasps the back of the chair for support*) Oh, dear!
Rose (*concerned*) Here, steady on!

Kesiah (*sitting again*) Get yourself a glass from the cupboard and come and sit down.

Rose does as she is bidden and then holds out her glass. Kesiah pours her a drink—rather unsteadily

Rose (*observing her closely*) I say! You've had a few!

Kesiah Nothing to do with you if I have. It's my gin and I buy it for drinking. Any objection?

Rose None. None at all. Best respects. (*She raises her glass and drinks*)

Kesiah As I remember it, you were going to bring me the address of the woman who buys second-hand clothes. (*There is now a certain deliberation about her speech*)

Rose I have it with me. Here it is. (*She produces a piece of paper which she hands to Kesiah*)

Kesiah (*studying the paper*) "Kate Donovan, Wardrobe Dealer." Well, I'll see if we can do business. No good leaving those clothes lying about waiting for the moths to get them.

Rose That's what I say. (*She drinks*) Might as well turn them into money.

Kesiah I suppose you know her well—this Kate Donovan.

Rose Let's put it this way—I've been going to her for a number of years.

Kesiah What's the news at *The Crown*?

Rose There isn't any. (*Recollecting*) Oh yes. Somebody said they saw Janey Johnson here in the yard pegging out clothes.

Kesiah (*furious*) "Saw Janey Johnson!" What do you mean—"saw Janey Johnson"?

Rose (*conciliatory*) I told them they couldn't have seen her and it couldn't have been her ghost—not in broad daylight.

Kesiah Let me tell you something—and you can pass it on to whoever it was. Janey Johnson is six feet under. I'll show you and then you'll know. (*She gets to her feet, not without difficulty, lurches over to the cellar door and wrenches it open*) Janey Johnson fell down these—(*pointing*)—steps to her death. She was in a desperate hurry to get something for Mrs Sumner. It was all dealt with at the Coroner's inquest. So will you tell them—all those who have nothing better to talk about at *The Crown*.

Rose Yes, I'll tell them. But I did know.

Kesiah (*coming over to her*) Then you should have told them. I don't want that lot starting tales about Janey Johnson or anything that happened here. Now or ever. (*She pokes Rose with her forefinger*) Remember that.

Rose (*wincing*) Yes, I will. (*Her expression changing*) It must have been that girl they saw. It must have been her pegging out the clothes.

Kesiah Of course it was. I've had about enough of you. Stay here. (*She storms out to the kitchen and returns with a large brown-paper parcel which she thrusts at Rose*) Here. Here's some of Janey Johnson's clothes. Take them and get out.

Rose I meant no harm. I was just telling you . . .

Kesiah You heard what I said—get out. And let it be a long time before you come here again.

Rose Very well. If that's the way you want it. I'm not one to stay where I'm not wanted. (*She moves towards the kitchen door and turns to Kesiah*) All I can say is that you're very touchy.

Kesiah We won't start on your shortcomings or we'll be here all night.

Kesiah hustles Rose, clutching her parcel, from the room and we hear the back door closed and bolted resoundingly. Kesiah comes back slowly into the room. Disturbed and angry, she mutters

Janey Johnson . . .

Kesiah walks over to the table and has just taken hold of the gin bottle when Janey's voice is heard

Janey's Voice When I looked out, I thought I saw Death himself standing there.

Kesiah rushes over to the cellar door and closes it, standing with her back to it

Kesiah And you did, didn't you? But you were too stupid to heed the warning.

From the kitchen comes Margaret's voice

Margaret's Voice I know as I stand here that there is a God and I know just as certainly that He will not allow you to live here for very long. Make the most of it, gipsy!

Kesiah And I'm doing just that! (*She moves into the centre of the room and glances first at the cellar door and then at the kitchen*) You can't frighten me—either of you. You're dead and you can't hurt me. I'm here to stay. (*She goes to the table, picks up the handbell and shakes it furiously*)

After a moment Deborah enters

Kesiah replaces the bell on the table

Deborah Has that woman gone?

Kesiah She has and she's never to set foot in this house again. Never, you understand?

Deborah Yes, missus. If you say so. I didn't like her—that's why I ran away. (*She regards Kesiah intently*) You look shaken up, missus.

Kesiah That woman upset me.

Deborah I know what you need. (*She goes to the table, pours a drink into Kesiah's glass and offers it to her*) Here.

Kesiah accepts it

Kesiah You've a good heart, Deborah. A kind heart. I hope nobody ever takes advantage of you because of it. (*She returns to her place at the table and sits*) Now you're going to have a drink with me.

Deborah But, missus, I don't . . .

Kesiah (*firmly*) You're going to have a drink with me. Do as you're told. Get yourself a glass from the cupboard.

Deborah does as she is bidden and stands, glass in hand, by the cupboard

Now come and sit down.

Deborah obeys. Kesiah pours some gin into Deborah's glass. Then she raises her own glass to Deborah

Good health, Deborah.

Deborah Good health to you, missus.

They drink. Deborah chokes and splutters. Kesiah laughs. Deborah sits holding her throat

Kesiah Maybe you shouldn't have drunk it neat—that's for old topers like myself. Go and get some water.

Deborah goes to the kitchen and returns with a jug of water

During her absence, Kesiah drinks and empties her glass

That's right. Now pour some water into your glass.

Deborah does so

Now try it.

Deborah first sips gingerly and then drinks. She puts down the glass

Better?

Deborah nods

You know what I'm going to do with you?

Deborah No, missus.

Kesiah I'm going to give you this room to yourself. (*Checking Deborah's reaction with upraised hand*) Yes, I am. I'm going to live in the drawing room in future. It's only right as I'm the mistress.

Deborah Yes, missus. (*She picks up the bottle and refills Kesiah's glass*)

Kesiah Thank you, Deborah. I can see we're going to get on well. I can trust you, Deborah.

Deborah Yes, missus.

Kesiah I'll show you something. Go to the cupboard and bring what you find in the corner on the bottom shelf.

Kesiah drinks. Deborah goes to the cupboard, rummages briefly and holds up the thong

Is this it, missus—this piece of old leather?

Kesiah Bring it here.

Deborah returns to the table and gives the thong to Kesiah. She sits and watches as Kesiah rises and stretches the thong between her hands

This has been a friend to me and never more so than on the first night I was here. Know what I did?

Deborah No, missus.

Kesiah I took this (*She snaps the thong*) and tied it across the bend of the cellar stairs.

Deborah Why did you do that, missus?

Kesiah I wanted Janey Johnson out of the way so I told her that her mistress needed her in the cellar—told her to hurry. She tripped over this and that was the end of Janey.

Kesiah tosses the thong onto the table, sits and studies Deborah who remains inscrutable

You shocked, Deborah?

Deborah No, missus. But I don't see why you wanted Janey Johnson out of the way.

Kesiah I calcu—calculated that Mrs Sumner would want me to stay if she was all alone and I was right—she did. She asked me to stay until she got a new housekeeper. I took good care to see she didn't get one.

Deborah How did you do that, missus?

Kesiah Frightened them away—every single one of them. And that wasn't all. There was a niece—a niece she was fond of and one she wanted to have this house.

Deborah (*puzzled*) But she left it to you, missus. You told me she left it to you.

Kesiah Too true she did. Mrs Sumner and the niece quarrelled and the niece kept writing to say how sorry she was. But Mrs Sumner never got the letters. Do you know why?

Deborah No, missus.

Kesiah (*laughing*) Because I burned them and I burned the letters Mrs Sumner gave me to post to her niece.

Deborah You'd got it all worked out, missus.

Kesiah I had that. Then I played my trump card—threatened to get out if she didn't leave me the house. So she did and soon after she died of one of her heart attacks.

Deborah And she never knew that the niece had written to her.

Kesiah Oh, Yes. I told her just before she died. I owed her that. She threatened me when I came here that first night. She cursed me before she died. But it made no difference. I've beaten her. (*She hugs herself*) I'm here snug and safe in my own house.

Deborah (*rising*) You're neither snug nor safe, Kesiah. And I don't think you'll stay very long in this house.

Deborah is suddenly a different person—alert and active. Kesiah looks up. She is startled and bewildered not only by the words but because the country accent has been replaced by an educated authoritative voice

Don't you know who I am?

Kesiah (*squinting up at her*) Who are you? I never saw you before in my life until I found you out there in the yard.

Deborah But you've heard of me, Kesiah . . .

Kesiah (*realization dawning*) Oh, that's it. You're the niece.

Clare That's right. I'm Clare Foster and I'm going to make good use of what you've told me.

Kesiah Oh no, you're not! (*She snatches up the thong as she rises to face Clare. She snaps the stretched thong menacingly between her hands*) Not on your life!

Dr Graham and another middle-aged woman appear in the doorway of the kitchen. The latter is Emmeline Martell and she is well-dressed and of formidable appearance

Clare Behind you, Kesiah! Behind you!

Kesiah (*smiling unpleasantly*) You don't catch me like that.

Emmeline You would do well to pay heed to her, gipsy.

Kesiah whirls round and, as she does so, Clare darts forward and snatches the thong from her. Kesiah looks from one to the other of the newcomers and her glance lingers disappointedly on Dr Graham

Kesiah So I was wrong to think of you as my friend, Doctor?

Dr Graham Yes, and wrong to think you had deceived me. I have been suspicious of you ever since Mrs Sumner died.

Kesiah Have you now? (*Staring at Emmeline*) And who are you? I don't think I've ever seen you before.

Emmeline It doesn't matter in the least whether you've seen me before or not. As it happens, I'm Emmeline Martell, the Vicar's wife.

Clare I'm so glad you came, Mrs Martell. (*She disposes of the thong by throwing it onto the armchair*)

Emmeline And I'm very pleased to think that, as witnesses, the Doctor and I will be instrumental in putting this creature where she can do no further mischief.

Kesiah A very Christian sentiment.

There is a loud knocking at the front door

Emmeline Ah, that will be Inspector Knight from Rye. I telephoned him
   before I left the Rectory. We've certainly got something to tell him—
   (*turning to Kesiah*)—especially you. I think the drawing room might be
   best, don't you, Clare?
Clare Oh, yes. Yes, of course.
Dr Graham Shall I let the Inspector in?
Emmeline Would you, please?

Dr Graham goes out

Right. We'll make our way to the drawing room. Come along, gipsy.
I shall be right behind you. Remember that. Right behind you.

*Kesiah begins to move towards the kitchen but then pauses and looks as if she
has made a startling discovery. She turns to Clare*

Kesiah Wait a moment—I've just realized who you are.
Clare But I told you . . .
Kesiah No, no. It's something else. You're the watcher in the shadow—the
   one old Cleo warned me about. I should have been looking out for you.

Kesiah goes out

Emmeline (*following her*) The creature is obviously unbalanced.

Emmeline goes out

*Left alone, Clare looks round the room, sees the thong, goes to the armchair,
and picks up the strip of leather. Experimentally, she flexes and stretches it
between her hands*

Emmeline (*off*) Come along Clare. The Inspector will want to speak to you.
Clare I'm coming. (*She looks again at the thong*) I'm just bringing a piece
   of evidence.

Clare goes out, as—

the CURTAIN falls

FURNITURE AND PROPERTY LIST

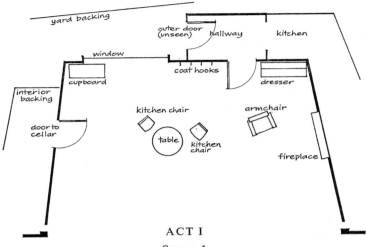

ACT I

SCENE 1

On stage: Circular table
2 kitchen chairs
Armchair
Dresser
Cupboard. *In it:* bottle of sherry, glasses
Coathooks. *On them:* shopping bag
On walls: cheap framed prints

Off stage: Thong (**Kesiah**)
Tray with glass of water, plate of bread and cheese (**Janey**)
Bottle of wine (**Janey**)
Plate of pie, knife, fork (**Janey**)
Lighted lantern (**Janey**)

Personal **Janey:** bunch of keys

SCENE 2

Strike: Sherry, dirty glass, tray of food and plates

Set: Room less tidy
Towel over kitchen chair
Used cup, saucer, plate, milk jug, sugar basin, teapot, jar of marmalade
Nelly's coat on hook
Tray on kitchen chair

Off stage: Split logs (**Nelly**)
Cloth (**Nelly**)
Purse containing sovereigns (**Margaret**)
Medical bag containing box of pills (**Dr Graham**)
Clothes basket of soiled linen (**Nelly**)
Unopened letter (**Kesiah**)

ACT II

Scene 1

Set: Gin bottle and glasses on table

Off stage: Glass of water **(Kesiah)**

Scene 2

Strike: Bottle and glasses
                Glass of water

Set: *On table:* 2 cups, 2 saucers, 2 plates, 2 knives, teapot, cream jug, sugar
                  bowl, cut cake
                In cupboard: gin bottle; check glasses
                On dresser: 2 parcels of silver

Off stage: Plate of bread and cheese; beaker of milk **(Kesiah)**
                Canvas bundle **(Deborah)**

Scene 3

Strike: Plate and milk beaker
                Bottle and glasses

Set: Bottle of gin and glass on table
                Handbell on table
                Thong in cupboard

Off stage: Piece of paper **(Rose)**
                Large brown-paper parcel **(Kesiah)**
                Jug of water **(Deborah)**

LIGHTING PLOT

Property fittings required: gas-light pendant
INTERIOR. A housekeeper's room. The same scene throughout

ACT I SCENE 1. Evening
To open: Gas fitting on. Dark outside
No cues

ACT I SCENE 2. Morning
To open: General effect of morning light
No cues

ACT II SCENE 1. Evening
To open: As Act I Scene 1
No cues

ACT II SCENE 2. Evening
To open: As previous scene
No cues

ACT II SCENE 3. Evening
To open: As previous scene
No cues